OVER 6000 YEARS AGO

IN THE STONE AGE

HAZEL MARY MARTELL

ILLUSTRATIONS BY CHRIS ROTHERO

A ZOË BOOK

A ZOË BOOK

Devised and produced by
Zoe Books Limited
15 Worthy Lane
Winchester
Hampshire SO23 7AB
England

First published in Great Britain by Zoe Books Limited, 15 Worthy Lane, Winchester, Hampshire SO23 7AB

A record of the CIP data is available from the British Library

Printed in Belgium

Design: Pardoe Blacker
Picture research: Sarah Staples
Illustrations: Chris Rothero

Photograph acknowledgements

The publishers wish to acknowledge, with thanks, the following photographic sources:

7, 11 Michael Holford; 15 Ronald Sheridan/Ancient Art and Architecture Collection; 18 Mick Sharp; 23 English Heritage; 26 British Museum

Contents

Hunting for Food

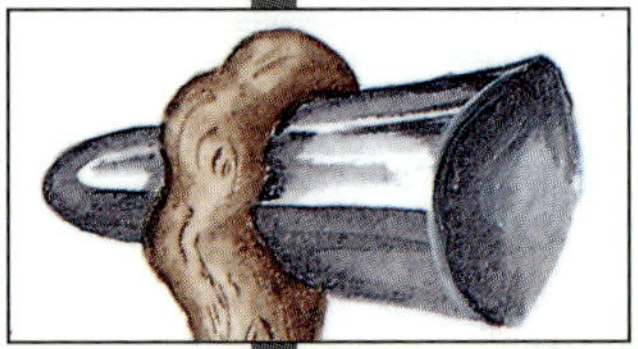

The Stone Age is the name given to the time before people found out how to use metals such as copper or iron. It is called the Stone Age because the people who lived then made their tools and weapons out of stone or wood. The Stone Age lasted for different lengths of time in different parts of the world. This book concentrates mainly on the Stone Age in Europe which lasted until around 1500 BC.

Stone Age people needed food, warmth and shelter to live. They gathered wild berries and plants to eat. They also hunted wild animals such as deer and the elephant-like mammoth.

When the Stone Age people were hunting large animals such as the mammoth, they hunted in groups. They used wooden spears and arrows which had sharp stone or flint points. The animals provided meat to eat and skins which were used for clothes and tent-coverings. Bones and antlers were used to make tools.

The people moved around, following the animals as they searched for food. Sometimes the people lived in tents or huts made from branches. In the coldest weather they sheltered in caves in rocks.

Tools and cave paintings

Stone Age people have left behind many of their tools and weapons. The earliest ones are stones that were sharpened against other stones to make a point or a cutting edge. These tools were probably held in the hand, but later tools were fastened to handles made from wood or from animal bones.

At places such as Dolni Vestonice in Czechoslovakia, piles of animal bones have been found. This tells us that the people who lived there over 25 000 years ago were skilled hunters. They might have dug pits or traps for the animals to fall into. In other places, animal bones have been found with an arrowhead or spearpoint still sticking in them.

Some Stone Age people also painted hunting scenes on the walls of their caves. Some of these paintings have been found in France and Spain. They are almost 20 000 years old. By studying these pictures, together with the things people made, called artefacts, archaeologists are able to tell us how people lived at different times during the Stone Age.

Some of the cave paintings show hunters using bows and arrows like these. Archaeologists have also found the remains of bows, and arrowheads which are still attached to wooden shafts.

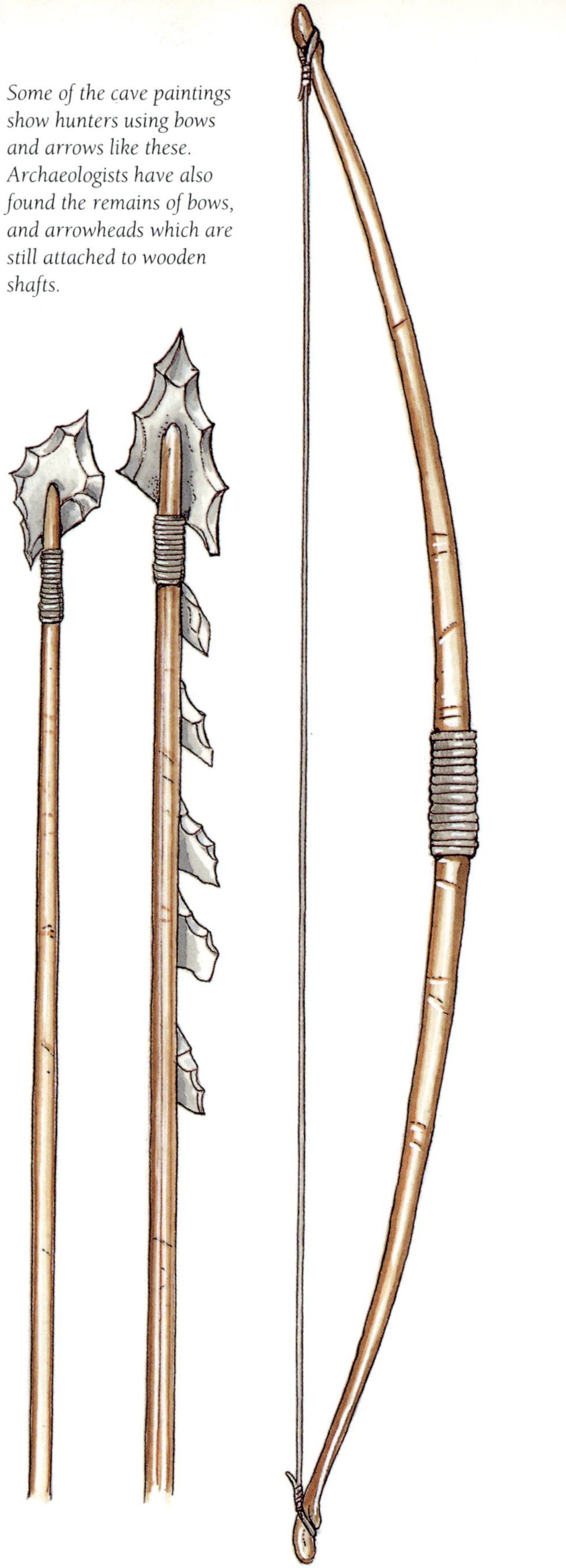

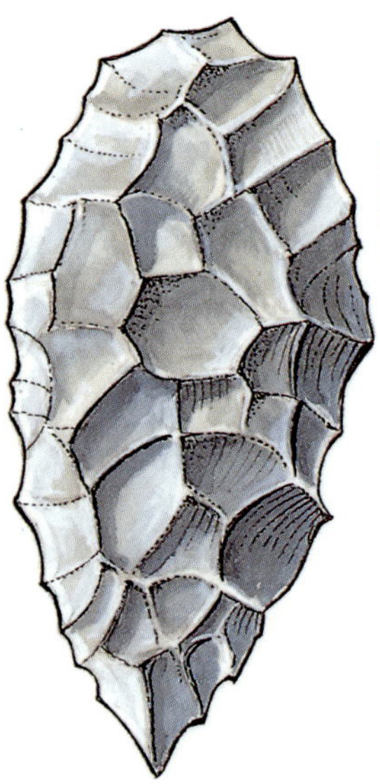

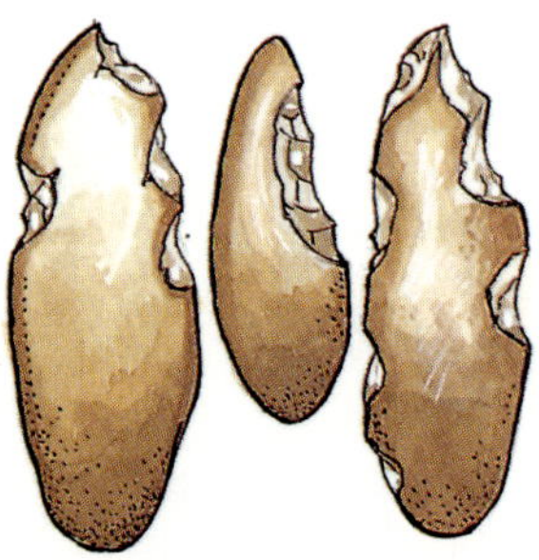

Stone Age people made clothes and tents from the skins of animals they caught. The large scraper on the left was used to clean the flesh from the skin. The skins were joined together by threading a strip of skin through holes made along the edge. The holes were made with pointed stones, like those above.

A painting of a bison on the wall of a cave at Altamira in Spain.

Evidence such as tools, weapons and bones show us where people lived, as well as how they lived. Soil is also important evidence. It contains the remains of insects, seeds and pollen which tell us what the climate was like, and what type of plants grew.

How important do you think hunting was to Stone Age people? Look for the clues.

HISTORY DETECTIVE

There were artists and craftworkers amongst the Stone Age people. In many places, as well as cave paintings, small clay animals have been found. Archaeologists think that these figures and the paintings may have been made to bring success to the hunters.

Paints were made from coloured earth, called ochre, mixed with animal fat. The colours were brown, yellow, orange, red and black. Brushes were made of animal hair.

Clearing the Land

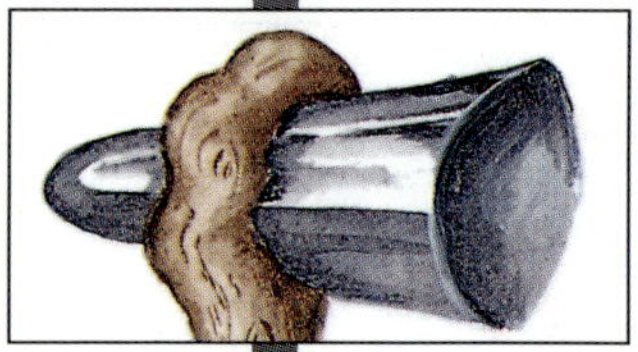

Ten thousand years ago the Ice Age was coming to an end in what is now called Europe. As the climate began to get warmer, the vegetation began to change. More trees grew and many areas were covered with thick forests. Some animals that were used to colder conditions, such as reindeer, moved, or migrated, north. Others, such as the mammoth, were not suited to the new environment and gradually died out, or became extinct.

Around the same time, the people who lived in the Middle East started to settle down and farm the land, instead of hunting animals for food. This idea very slowly spread to Europe over thousands of years.

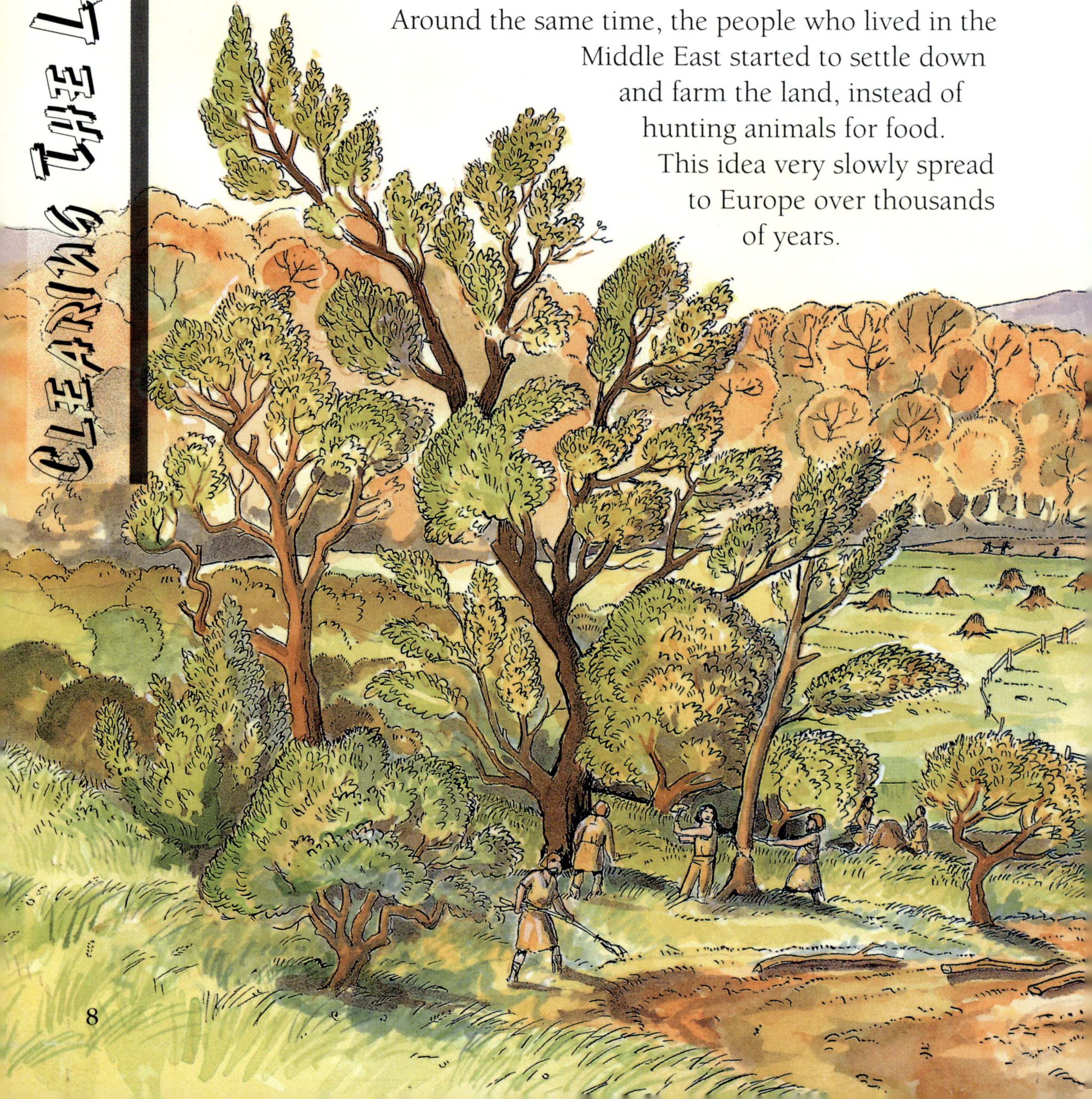

The first farmers started by domesticating some of the wild animals, such as pigs and cattle, and keeping them for meat, milk and skins. They also kept sheep and goats and, at a later date, used manure from these animals to help fertilize the ground.

The farmers also planted some of the seeds they had gathered. However, because the land was now covered in forests, trees had to be cleared before fields could be made. The Stone Age people made good use of the trees they cut down.

The tree trunks and larger branches were used to build shelters or make canoes. The smaller branches were piled up around the tree stumps and burned. The ash from these fires fertilized the soil, which was then dug and raked. When the tree stumps rotted away, the land could be ploughed.

People, animals and crops need water as well as food. Stone Age people often chose to clear the land near a river or a lake. They caught fish to eat and they could also travel by water. It was easier to move around by water than through thick forest.

To make fire, Stone Age people rubbed two pieces of flint together over some dried grass. When the flints made a spark, it would set the grass on fire.

Tools for clearing the land

Stone Age farmers used stone axes to chop down the trees. The edge of the axehead was sharpened against another stone before being fixed on a wooden or bone handle. People used a digger or pick to break up the soil. Like the axe, the head of the pick was made of stone. Some pick handles, or shafts, were wooden, others were made from deer antlers.

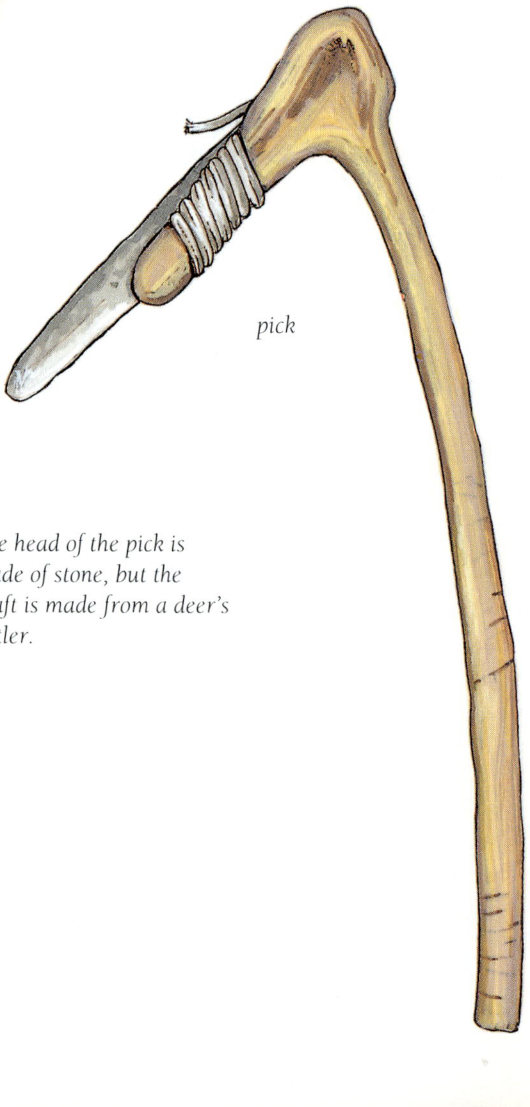

pick

The head of the pick is made of stone, but the shaft is made from a deer's antler.

How old?

When plants and animals are alive, they absorb a substance called carbon dioxide. In this there is a small amount of Carbon 14. This is a form of carbon that is radioactive. When something dies, the Carbon 14 in it starts to decay. Scientists know the rate at which Carbon 14 decays. This means that if they can measure how much Carbon 14 there is left in something like a piece of wood, scientists can work out how old it is. This test is known as radio-carbon dating. It works best on objects up to 10 000 years old.

Tools for boat-building

Two of the most important woodworking tools were the adze and the burin. They were both used to hollow out tree trunks. The adze could cut out large chunks of wood, while the burin carved out smaller pieces. The burin was like a chisel.

Stone Age people probably started clearing new land after the harvest. This would mean they had food for the winter and seeds to plant for the next year's crop. The picture on page 8-9 shows they had several different uses for the trees they chopped down. Can you find six of them? How do we know that people had to clear the forest before they could farm? Why did the farmers like to clear land which was near water? Look for the clues.

HISTORY DETECTIVE

The adze and the axe were both made of stone, and their shafts were made from wood. The small tools on the right were held in the hand and used as hammers or chisels.

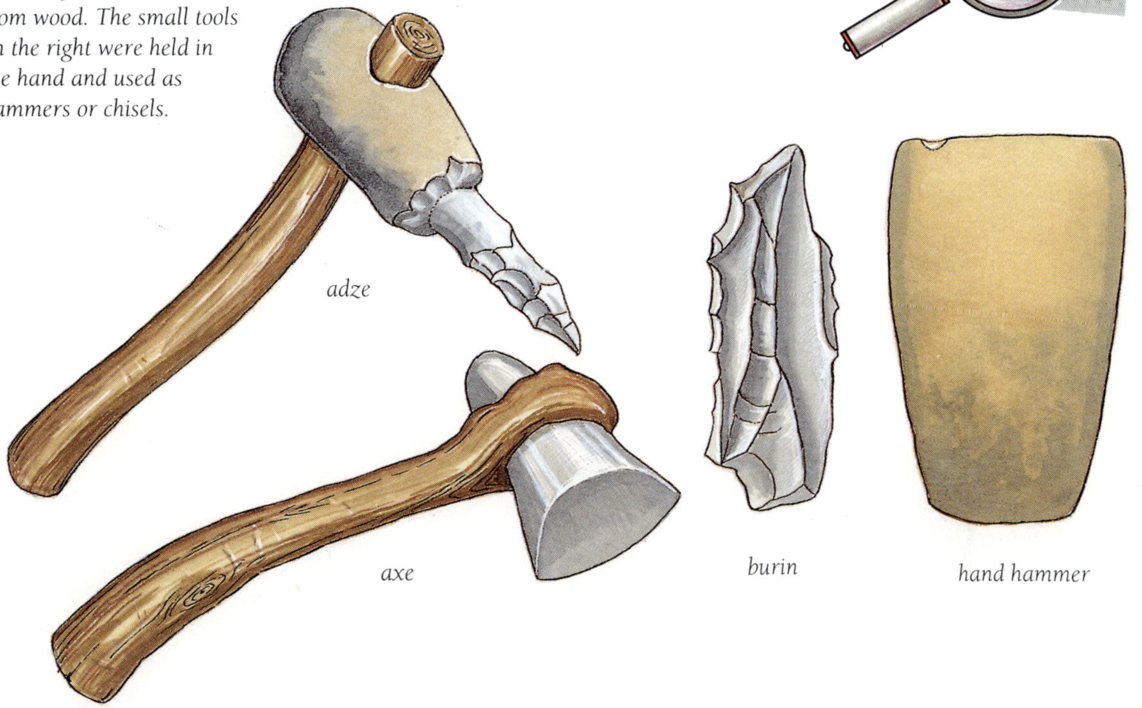

This digging paddle was found in England. It is 51 centimetres (20 inches) long and made of wood.

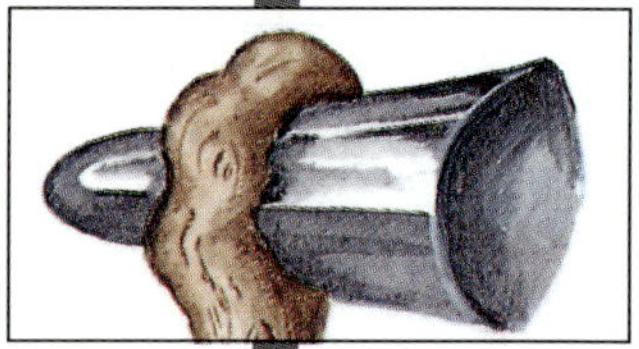

This picture of a Stone Age settlement is based on evidence found at Burgaschi in Switzerland. Archaeologists think that the site was occupied about 5500 years ago. The ground on the site was marshy, so the people cut about 3000 wooden stakes, or piles, from the forest and pushed them into the ground. The stakes made a firm base for the houses and pathways.

More wood was used to construct a fence around the buildings. This enclosure was 50 metres (55 yards) long and 10 metres (11 yards) wide. The pathways between the buildings were also made of wood.

Near the enclosure at Burgaschi there was a flat piece of ground where crops were grown. A few seeds were found on the site by archaeologists and these were identified as barley and a type of wheat called emmer wheat. These crops were harvested using stone sickles. Some seeds were put aside to plant for the next year's crops. Most of the seeds were crushed into flour on a large, round, flat stone.

The people also gathered wild fruit, nuts and berries from the forest. They hunted deer and wild boar, and fished in the lake. They kept pigs, sheep and cattle for meat, skins and milk.

Archaeological evidence

The marshy ground at Burgaschi kept some of the wood and other artefacts from rotting away. Archaeologists found the remains of upright posts and boards which had formed part of the house walls. They also found some wooden roof supports. These supports were strong enough to hold up a grass or reed roof.

Reeds grew at the edge of the lake. They could be used to make a type of thatch for the roofs and to weave into baskets. Thin branches were woven into lengths of wickerwork, to make fences or house walls.

There was also evidence that flax was grown at Burgaschi. The stems of this plant contain strong, thin fibres, which can be spun into thread. The thread would be woven into linen cloth. Clothes were made from linen, as well as from wool and animal skins.

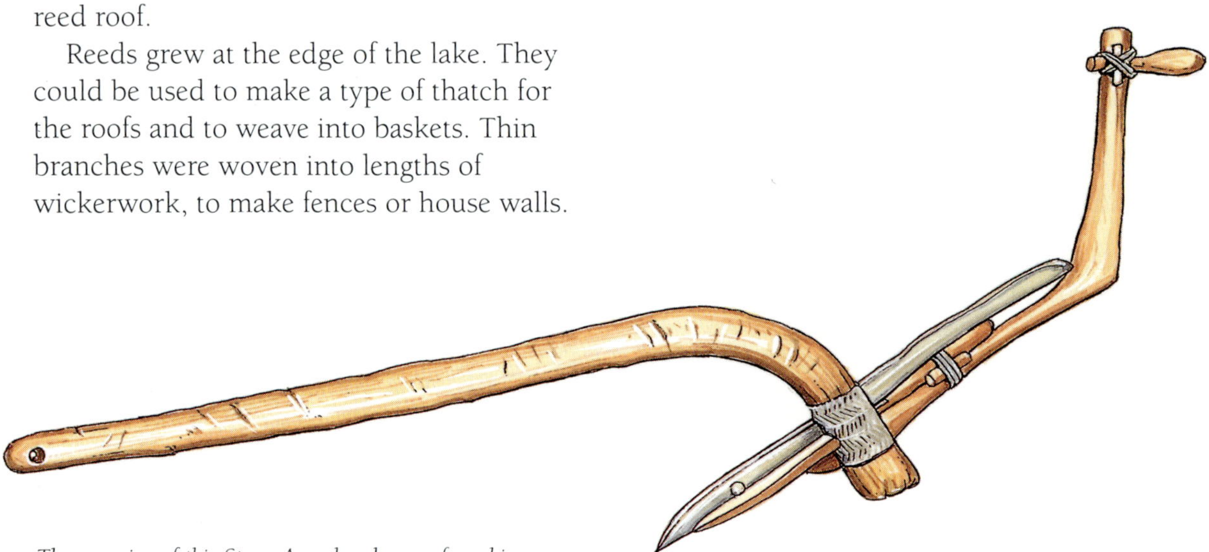

The remains of this Stone Age plough were found in Denmark. It was made of wood, but its point was made of stone. This plough made one furrow at a time.

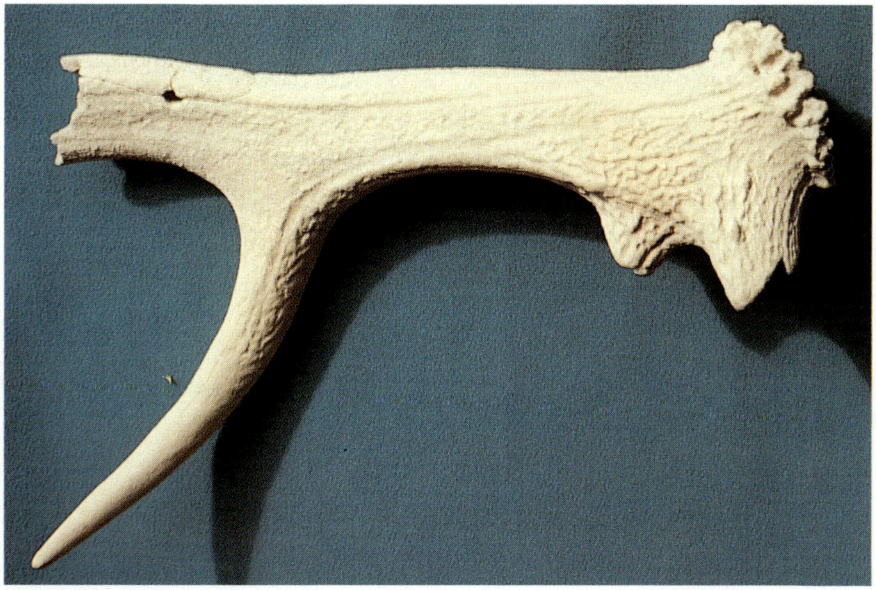

This pick is made from the antler of a reindeer. There was a good supply of antlers as all deer shed them every year. Other parts of animals were also made into tools for farming. For example, the shoulder blades of cattle made good spades for digging the soil.

Just how much the early farmers still relied on hunting and gathering has been worked out by archaeologists in the Tehuacan valley in Mexico. About 7000 years ago the people there started growing crops like corn and beans during the summer. In the autumn they grew avocados and picked wild fruits, while in the winter they went hunting. From evidence found in their excavations, archaeologists estimate that the diet of the people of Tehuacan was made up of 52 per cent wild plants, 34 per cent meat and only 14 per cent products they had grown themselves.

What crops did the people at Burgaschi grow, and what food did they find in the forests? What meat did they eat?

HISTORY DETECTIVE

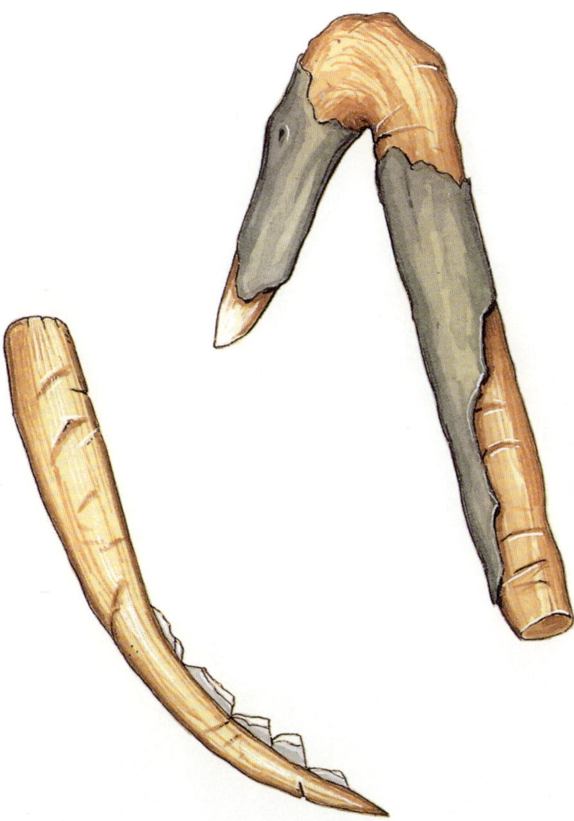

The sickle on the left was used for cutting crops. It was made from wood with sharpened pieces of a hard stone called flint stuck into it to make a blade. The hoe above it was used to break up the soil.

At Home

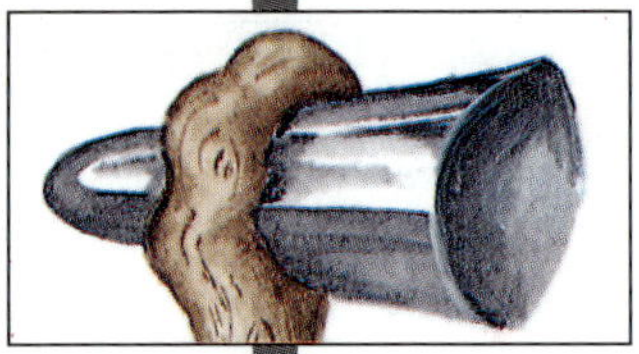

This picture of a Stone Age house is based on evidence found at Avebury in England. There were a lot of trees at Avebury, so the houses were made of wood. Most of the wood has now rotted away, but marks in the soil show where the house walls stood. Archaeologists have measured marks like these at different sites. They have found that a Stone Age house in Britain, 6000 years ago, was usually about 8 metres (8.75 yards) long and 4.5 metres (5 yards) wide.

No wooden furniture has been found at Avebury, but in other places where houses were built of stone, they had stone cupboards and stone bedframes. However, scientists who study skeletons think that people squatted rather than sat, so perhaps they never made chairs or stools.

All the daily activities took place in one room. These included preparing, cooking and eating food, grinding corn for flour, spinning wool and weaving it into cloth. Animal skins were scraped, stretched and made into clothes. Children played and were looked after. There were no windows in the house. The only light came from the open doorway or from the fire.

Although no furniture has survived in the Avebury area, some of the pottery has done. The pots are in different shapes and sizes, and some still contained the remains of the food which had been cooked or stored in them.

Stone Age food

Archaeologists have tested, or analyzed, the remains of the food to find out more about what Stone Age people ate and how they cooked their food.

The people cooked food in several different ways. They usually roasted or grilled their meat over the fire. Sometimes they wrapped the meat in leather and buried it in the glowing embers of a slow fire to bake. They heated water by dropping hot stones into it, so that they could boil food.

Flour was a very important part of the people's diet. After the grain had been crushed into flour, the flour was mixed with water and shaped into loaves. These loaves were baked in clay ovens.

In places where there were lots of stones lying on top of the ground, people used them to make things for their houses. This Stone Age house at Skara Brae in the Orkney Islands still has a cupboard and a bed made of stone. In the middle of the floor is the stone hearth where the fire burned.

Scientists have also tested the clay pots to find out how they were made. Small pots were shaped or moulded by hand from a ball of wet clay. Larger pots were made by coiling lengths of clay around on top of each other.

Clay was also used for making the weights, or whorls, for the spindles which Stone Age people used to spin wool into thread. The spindles were made of wood or bone. Larger clay weights held the threads straight when cloth was woven on a wooden frame called a loom.

These thick clay pots have been reconstructed from evidence found at Windmill Hill near Avebury. Some pots had patterns scratched on the sides. Others had handles to make them easier to lift.

This woman is making clothes from an animal skin. Twenty thousand years have passed since the time of the mammoth hunters, but she still has to prick holes in the edge of the skin with a stone. Instead of threading a strip of animal skin through the holes, however, she now uses a bone needle to sew with a thread made from an animal sinew.

HISTORY DETECTIVE

How do you know that the house on page 16-17 must have been dark and smoky sometimes?

What kinds of activities might have been done outside in good weather? Why would this have been better than doing them inside the house?

Mining And Making Tools

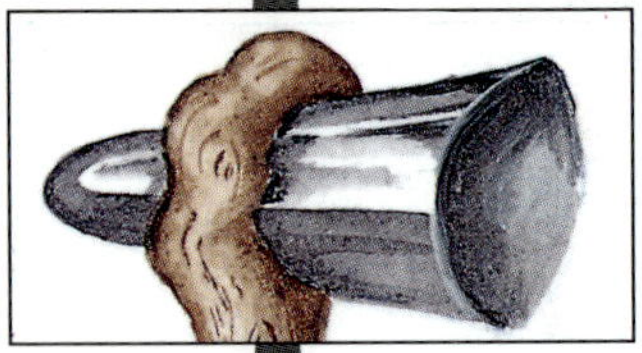

Stone Age people in Europe soon discovered that flint was the best type of stone for making tools and weapons. This was because it could be chipped with another stone or with a bone hammer. Flint also splits and flakes easily, leaving a thin, sharp edge. Tools and weapons such as knives, scrapers, axes and arrowheads were made from flint. Some flint came from stones on the ground, but there were a lot more beneath the surface.

People began to dig down into the ground to find more flintstone. There were flint mines at places such as La Spienne in Belgium and at Grimes Graves in Norfolk, England. The miners dug a pit or shaft down into the ground. At the bottom of the shaft they dug tunnels or galleries into the rock face. They did not know how to prop up the roofs so the galleries were not very high. There was always the danger of the roof falling in.

The miners probably put the pieces of flint, called nodules, into leather bags or wicker baskets. Then the baskets were pulled or carried up to the surface.

Grimes Graves

The first archaeological dig, or excavation, at Grimes Graves took place in 1868. In one of the grassy hollows on the site there was a mine shaft. It was about 12 metres (45 feet) deep, and it was full of stones. Since 1868 between 700 and 800 shafts and pits have been found at Grimes Graves. Archaeologists have worked out that it took about 40 days to dig the flint from the galleries at the bottom of the shaft. When the miners dug a new shaft, they used the waste to fill in the pits they were no longer using.

The miners' digging tool was a pick, made from the antler of a deer. Many of these trimmed antlers have been found on the site. Shovels were made from the shoulder blades of deer and cattle. The miners used the shovels to clear away waste earth and stones.

The workers who shaped the flint into tools were called flint knappers. They broke up the large nodules with a heavy hammerstone. Then they chipped off thin flakes to make small, sharp tools such as arrowheads, blades and chisels. They shaped the thicker pieces of stone into axeheads.

Although flint was used in many places during the Stone Age, the stone from one area is usually slightly different from that in another area. Archaeologists can test the stones to find out where the flint came from. Axeheads from Grimes Graves have been found up to 300 kilometres (188 miles) away.

These men are knapping, or chipping, nodules of flint into tools. In wet weather they worked in an abandoned part of the mine.

Some miners used stone lamps like this one, made from a piece of hollowed-out chalk filled with animal fat. The figure below was found in Grimes Graves. It is thought to be a goddess.

HISTORY DETECTIVE

Archaeologists have found lots of deer antlers which were used as tools at Grimes Graves. They have studied these antlers carefully and have found that between 100 and 150 of them were used to dig out each shaft. The archaeologists have worked out that it would take about 100 days for a team of 20 people to dig a shaft deep enough to reach the best flint. Both digging the shaft and removing the flint were dangerous jobs.

Look at the picture on page 20-21. Everything is going well there, but can you imagine what the dangers might be? Why do you think the miners used picks made from deer antlers, instead of making them from stone? What sort of tools were made from the flint found at Grimes Graves?

This picture shows some of the galleries at Grimes Graves. The galleries were dug out around 2000 BC, but the metal supports are modern.

THE FIRST TOWNS

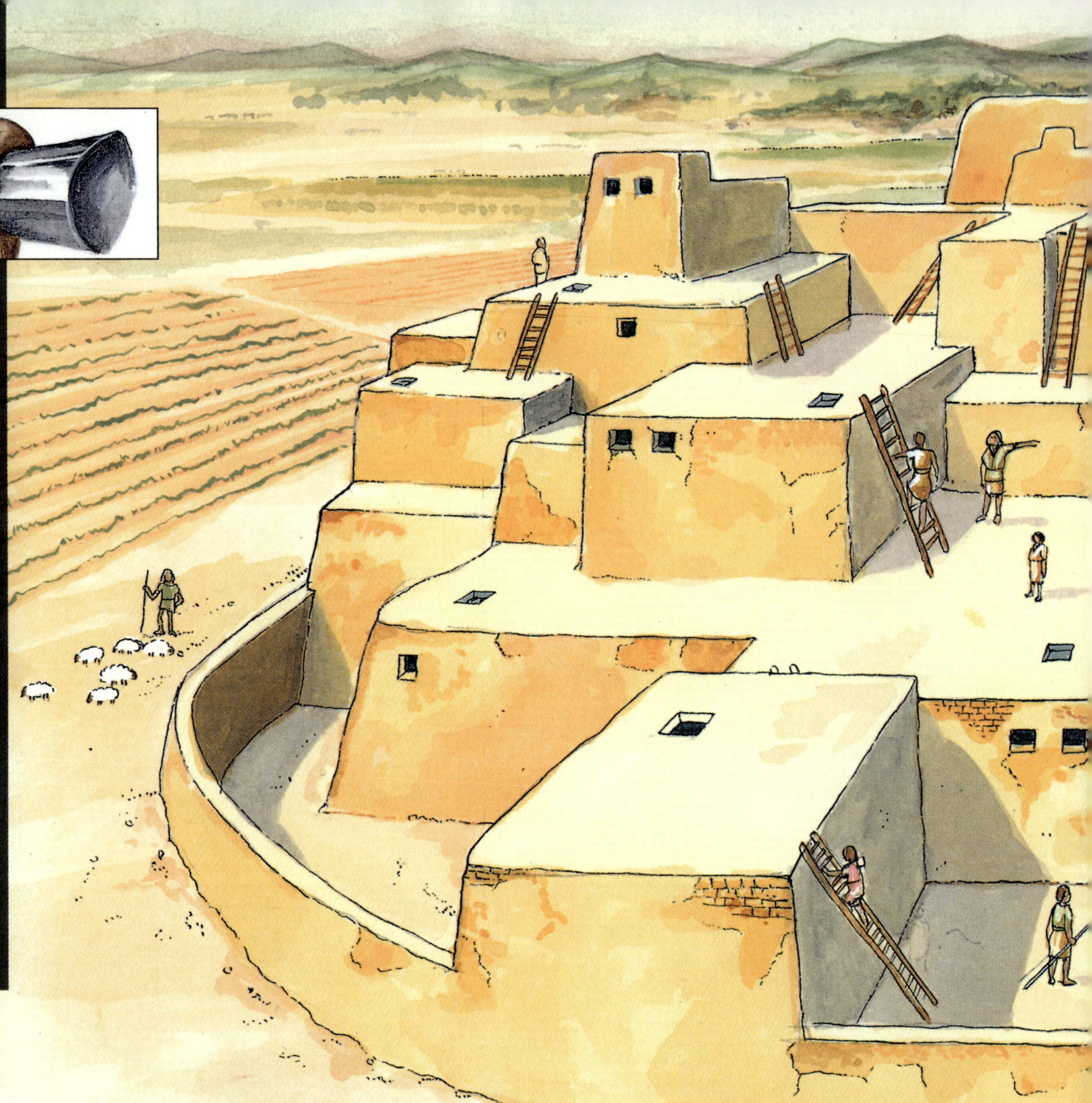

One of the first known towns is Catal Huyuk, in what is now called Turkey. The people of Catal Huyuk were skilled potters and weavers. The town grew from a smaller village because the people produced goods which other people wanted and traded them over long distances. This picture shows how the town may have looked, about 6000 years ago.

The people of Catal Huyuk built their houses very close together. There were no streets. The houses were made of mud-bricks and plaster. Most houses had two floors, or storeys, under a flat roof. There were no doors, but ladders have

been found which suggest that the people went in and out of their houses through a hole in the roof. The houses had a hearth, an oven and a fuel stove.

At this time there may have been about 1000 houses and up to 6000 people in Catal Huyuk.

In the fields around the town the people grew wheat, barley, peas and lentils. They probably grew grapes and walnuts, and gathered nuts, almonds and crab apples from the nearby hills. They hunted deer, wild boar, hares and birds, and they kept cattle, sheep and goats.

Catal Huyuk

The builders of Catal Huyuk made the house walls out of mud. The roofs were made of branches which were then covered with reeds or straw and a layer of mud. Archaeologists have found skeletons with broken bones, which suggest that perhaps the people sometimes missed their footing when they were climbing the ladders into or out of their houses.

This marble figure of a woman was found at Catal Huyuk. It is almost 8000 years old.

The houses at Catal Huyuk were built from bricks made of mud. They were moulded by hand and dried in the sun until they were hard. When the walls were complete, they were covered in smooth plaster.

Many tools and weapons found at Catal Huyuk were made of volcanic rock. This rock, called obsidian, is hard and can be polished to look like black glass. Obsidian was used to make the mirrors which were buried with some of the women. Goods made of obsidian were popular with traders.

Pottery was found in every layer of ground which was excavated at the town. Wood was also used for making large dishes and boxes, while straw and reeds made floor-mats and baskets with lids.

Clothes were made from animal skins, and the people were skilled at weaving cloth from wool. Traders came to exchange goods such as flints or shells for the goods the people made. They did not use money. By this time the people of Catal Huyuk were beginning to use lead and copper to make beads and trinkets. When people began to use these metals to make tools and weapons on a large scale, the Stone Age would come to an end.

We do not know much about religion in Catal Huyuk, but in some shrines statues have been found which show a goddess with a baby, a bull, a leopard or a ram.

Archaeologists have also found evidence which suggests that when people died their bodies were left on platforms near the towns. Birds such as vultures would clean the flesh from the bones. Then the bones were buried beneath the houses. Men usually died at about 34, while women died when they were about 30 years old. Some skeletons show signs of arthritis, while others had head wounds.

HISTORY DETECTIVE

There is evidence that the people of Catal Huyuk traded goods over a wide area. Amongst other things which archaeologists have found there are necklaces made from shells which came from the Mediterranean Sea.

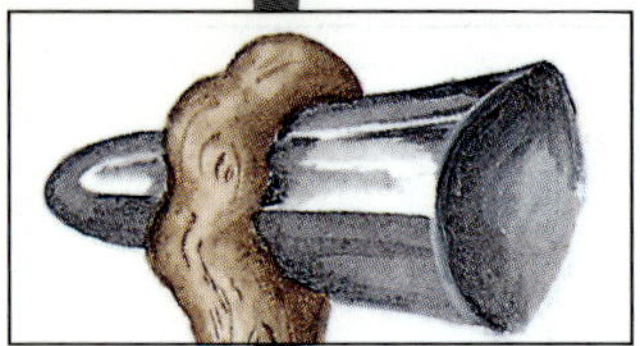

Time Line

BC	(before the birth of Christ)
27 000–23 000	The site at Dolni Vestonice is inhabited
18 000	Wall paintings made in caves at Lascaux, France
10 000	The end of the Ice Age in Europe. People gradually move further north as the temperature increases
9000	Farming begins in the Middle East
7000	Catal Huyuk growing into a town
6500	Farming begins in south-east Europe and gradually spreads north and west from there
4000	Farming spreads as far as southern England
2800	In southern England, work starts on the stone circle now known as Stonehenge
2000	Mining for flint at Grimes Graves in Norfolk, England Houses built at Skara Brae in the Orkney Islands to the north of Scotland As people learn to use metals, the Stone Age gradually gives way to the Bronze Age throughout Europe

AD	(*Anno Domini* which means 'in the year of our Lord')
1868	Exploration of some of the mines at Grimes Graves
1879	Discovery of the cave paintings at Altamira in Spain
1940	Discovery of the cave paintings at Lascaux in France
1950	Radio-carbon dating and other scientific methods used to give accurate dates to many objects from the past

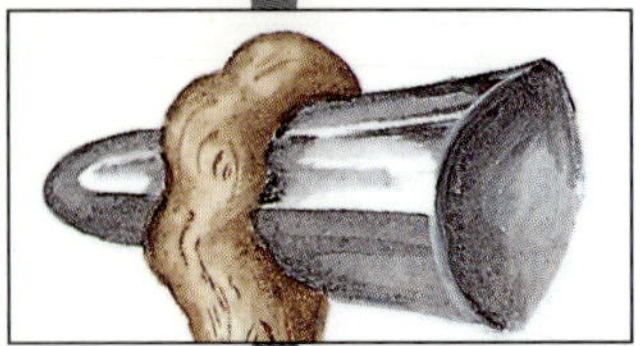

GLOSSARY

adze: a chopping tool with a slightly curved blade, used in woodworking

analyze: to study something very carefully to find how it was made and what it was made from

archaeologist: a person who finds out about the past by discovering and studying objects which were made then

artefact: any object which was made by people

arthritis: a disease of the joints which still shows up in skeletons after people have died

avocado: the rough-skinned, pear-shaped fruit of the avocado tree

bison: a type of cattle, now found only in protected herds

boar: a type of hairy pig. Those living in the wild could be very fierce

burin: a chisel-shaped tool used for chipping and engraving wood and stone

Carbon 14: a form of carbon which is radioactive. It is found in the carbon dioxide which is absorbed by all living things. When something dies, the Carbon 14 in it decays at a known rate

embers: small pieces of wood which are still burning in the bottom of a fire when the flames have died out

enclosure: a piece of land surrounded by a fence

excavation: clearing away or digging down into the ground, to find buildings or artefacts left behind by people who once lived there

flax: a blue-flowered plant which is grown for the fibres in its stems. These can be spun into a yarn called linen

flint knappers: people who took pieces of flint and chipped them into tools and weapons

gallery: a low, underground passage which was dug out by miners looking for flint

graze: to eat grass which is growing

Ice Age: one of the periods when ice from the North Pole spread south to cover much of the northern world. The Ice Age ended around 10 000 BC

loom: a frame on which thread, or yarn, is woven into cloth. In the Stone Age the loom was made from wood and the vertical threads were weighted down with stones

mammoth: an animal like a very large elephant with a hairy coat and curved tusks. It is now extinct

migrate: to move from one place to another, usually in search of food

moulding: shaping wet clay by hand

nodules: lumps of flint as they occur in nature

pick: a tool used for breaking up the ground

pile: a wooden stake driven into the ground to support a building

pollen: a fine, powdery substance which comes from flowers. Small grains of it can remain in the soil for centuries and then be identified by archaeologists

radio-carbon dating: a method of finding out how old certain objects are by measuring the amount of Carbon 14 left in them

settle: to live in one place, not moving around all the time in search of food

shaft: (1) the straight handle of a tool such as a pick (2) the opening which is dug into the ground at a mine

sickle: a cutting tool with a curved sharp edge. It was used to harvest crops

spindle: a stick or rod which is used to draw out threads from wool

storeys: floors or levels in a building

tundra: an area where most of the soil is permanently frozen. The top soil thaws a little in summer when mosses and small trees can grow

whorl: a weight attached to the bottom of a spindle to make it spin evenly and produce a smooth yarn

wickerwork: twigs, especially from the willow tree, which are woven or plaited together

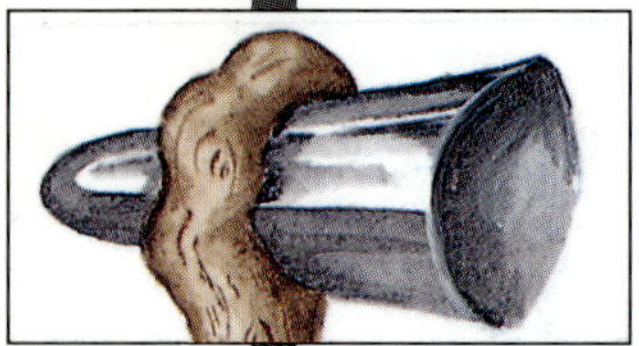

INDEX

PRINTED IN BELGIUM BY proost INTERNATIONAL BOOK PRODUCTION

DB Bitter
WARRIORS

POWER LEAGUE

Richard Becht and Dean Bell

AURUM PRESS

Page 1: Hitting the hills; getting ready to play. The Auckland Warriors in training before their 1995 Winfield Cup debut.
Page 2: Warriors second rower Tony Tatupu takes on the North Sydney defence.
Page 3: Tackling the league way... wrapping up both the man and the ball.
Page 4 (left): Wigan's play-maker Shaun Edwards.
Page 5 (opposite): Ricky Stuart, Canberra's magician.
Page 6: It's not easy to 'monster' Newcastle prop Paul Harragon, but North Sydney tacklers are doing their best.
Page 8: The fullback's ultimate test — taking the high ball. Penrith's Matt Adamson accomplishes the mission, just!
Page 9: Rugby league legend Mal Meninga taking a power of stopping, as usual.
Pages 10 and 11: Try time! Warriors centre Tea Ropati is the centre of affection after touching down against Western Suburbs.

First published in the United Kingdom by Aurum Press Limited, 25 Bedford Avenue, London WC1B 3AT, England, in association with David Bateman Ltd, Tarndale Grove, Albany Business Park, North Shore, Auckland, New Zealand

A CIP catalogue record for this book is available from the British Library

ISBN 1 85410 386 5

Design by Errol McLeary
Photographs supplied by Sportsphoto Agency and the archives of Fotopacific, sports photo agency and library.
Typeset in 11.5/13 Palatino
Printed in Hong Kong through Colorcraft Ltd

10
CITIBAN
13

CONTENTS

DB
Bitter

DB
Bitter
ANSETT

THE PLAY THE BALL

The play the ball movement is designed to keep play flowing rather than hold it up as happens in scrums or rucks [in rugby union], so all players should help exploit this advantage our game has by learning how to do it efficiently.

Rod Reddy (Australian International, 1978–82)

All sports have their distinguishing and distinctive characteristics. In rugby league it is unmistakably 'the play the ball', an action which is generic to the game and most obviously differentiates the two rugby codes. You can't watch a game without noticing the way players pop the ball between their legs, standing up to rake it back with the foot to a waiting dummy half. Rugby league wouldn't be rugby league without its play the ball. In a normal game of rugby league a player with a heavy work rate, like a prop, hooker or second rower, might play the ball between 30 and 35 times a match. Halfbacks, who tend to be the pivot and focus of an attack, aren't often caught or tackled in possession so they might perform the same act just a handful of times in a game, sometimes not at all.

Yet while it is an activity or skill that is central to the game it is often taken for granted. Certainly in the last few years, there

Opposite: With the ball about to be played, Cronulla's Andrew Neave first sights where his runners are before clearing the ball.

Right: Props and second rowers will usually play the ball more than other players at top level. They're the ones generally required to hit the ball up on early tackles and look for quick play the balls to allow the attack to gain some forward momentum. Warriors prop Gavin Hill (right) has done that against Brisbane, allowing hooker Duane Mann to clear the ball quickly from dummy half. Notice how Hill has also walked forward as he's played the ball, looking to shield Mann from the first marker.

has been a slightly blasé attitude from players and referees to its part in the game.

The intention of the play the ball is that a tackled player ought to be able to stand, once the referee has declared him held, and play or roll the ball back with his foot.

There are various technicalities involved.

- The tackled player must place the ball on the ground to play it back, at which time the opponent marking him can use his foot to strike for or rake the ball back on his side of the play the ball area.
- When playing the ball, the tackled player ought to be facing the opposition's goal line and be square on to the marker.
- The ball can't be played from a side on position, nor should it be played away from the area where the player was judged to be held (to advance a pace or two before playing the ball, which players often successfully try, is technically illegal).
- Playing the ball back with the hands is prohibited. But should the tackled player find no one marking him when he rises to play the ball, then he can tap the ball ahead, pick it up and advance the football as far as he can.

Opposite: The play the ball technique — the act which sets rugby league apart — restarts play after a tackle. As it is likely to feature around 350 times in a Winfield Cup match, it's an action all players need to perfect. Newcastle forward Tony Butterfield is doing everything right; leaning forward having placed the ball on the ground and rolled it back with his foot.

Left: Manly centre Danny Moore protects the ball as he plays it, leaning over and stepping forward as he does so. That way he all but eliminates the chance of the marker striking at the ball in an attempt to steal it.

10
the

That is how the play the ball should be. The reality of league in the '90s is that there is often an anything-goes attitude about the play the ball at the highest level. To a degree, referees, coaches and players have a similar rationale; they want to see the game played at the fastest pace possible and one way of achieving this is to adopt a tolerant view over the play the ball area. This means that some technical breaches of the rules are now conveniently overlooked.

One of the most obvious breaches can be seen in just about any Winfield Cup match — and it has caught on in England. This is when a tackled player plants the ball the moment he is tackled and as he tries to get to his feet he makes to play the ball in a far from upright stance. The tackler or tacklers often have not had sufficient time to get off the tackled player and invariably find themselves penalised for holding down in the tackle. If you were to isolate one player who is a master of this tactic, you would quickly pick out Canterbury-Bankstown's Kiwi centre Jarrod McCracken, who uses his enormous strength to shed tacklers, plants the ball and makes to play it back almost in one motion. It is an art which has served to give Canterbury-Bankstown (now the Sydney Bulldogs) a decided edge in getting a roll on in attack; other sides have been similarly successful.

Playing the ball properly is the first priority, but clearing the ball after it has been played is equally important. It's an area demanding expertise, and in almost every side the hooker is expected to provide it. Since his test debut in 1989, Duane Mann (above left) has provided key service from dummy half for the Kiwis, and Lee Jackson (above right) has developed into an expert all-round hooker for Great Britain. Here he is about to deliver a copy-book off-the-ground pass from dummy half against Australia in 1994.

Above: Penrith hooker Danny Farrar is captured in a perfect pose in the Winfield Cup, his weight over his left leg as he pivots to clear the ball to a runner.

Above right: Brian Noble captained Great Britain as long ago as 1984 (when he ended his test career), but he was still doing duty as a first division hooker for Wakefield Trinity at the start of the 1994–95 English season. Once again, the delivery technique for clearing the ball seems to be spot on.

You could easily argue the tackled player is not playing the ball correctly, yet it is the tackler who is often penalised for not getting off the tackled player quickly enough.

Many players are also guilty of ignorance in how to play the ball properly. Perhaps they were not well coached when they first started league and so they have developed bad habits. Players sometimes fail to protect themselves and the ball adequately when they stand to play the ball, leaving themselves wide open to expert poachers, like Ian Roberts and, until he retired, Ben Elias. However, to strike for the ball when you are marking a tackled player is a high-risk occupation. Strike too early and you are liable to be penalised. Should you strike legally and make contact with the ball but fail to win it, you know the tackle count will restart at nought for the team in possession.

I'm not a fan of players being able to strike for the ball. In fact, I would like to see the practice banned. A player, when tackled, should be able to stand without interference and play the ball. Striking for it only serves to slow the game down and it can be messy.

Assuming players have well-honed play the ball techniques, it is one area of the game that can make or break a team. Without

While the hooker will always try to be at dummy half to collect the ball, this is not always possible. All players have to be ready to move in to clear the ball if necessary.

Above left: It's not unusual to find a prop like Glenn Lazarus, here flicking out a pass in the 1992 World Cup final against Great Britain at Wembley, turning up if his hooker is not around.

Above right: A centre doing the duties after the ball's been played. This time it's Castleford's Richie Blackmore.

Right: Wigan's Denis Betts has played the ball, and it's his centre and captain Dean Bell who is at dummy half firing out a sweet pass.

quick play the balls even the sharpest attacking unit will falter; if the ball is slow to be played after a big break, and then slow to be cleared, any advantage will soon be nullified. To make each set of six tackles work for you, you need swift play the balls and slick service to extract genuine value and benefit from every attacking raid.

Fortunately, today's referees are keen to protect the side carrying the football; they are intent on ensuring attacking sides have the best chance possible to keep an attack going and, to that end, they have cleaned up the play the ball area remarkably well. Any tackler who errs slightly on the side of slowing play down by taking his time to get off a tackled player now knows he risks time in the 'sin bin' for a professional foul; and that is as it should be.

Because a Winfield Cup side can expect to have the ball for up to 250 tackles or more in a game, the play the ball is critical to the entire game plan. Do things well around that area and you'll be on the way.

The play the ball, because of its repetitive and ever-present part in the game, is focal to launching attacks. While many attacks and moves happen well away from the play the ball, the increased space around that area, through the 10-metre rule, now provides a wider range of options to attack close to the ruck.

It is from that area that teams work their switches in play, even something fairly straightforward like the playmaker — usually the halfback — lining up as receiver on the openside but, as the ball is being played, altering the point of the attack by shadowing across to the shortside or blindside to receive the football. Basic but effective, when the play the ball is tidy.

But maximising the value of efficient play the ball techniques is also dependent on strict refereeing. With the introduction of the 10-metre rule, the scope to attack has been increased, but only if referees police the rule fairly. With quick play the balls and the referee enforcing the 10-metre distance, gains on attack can be enormous.

On the reverse side, defence around the play the ball is just as crucial. Coaches today talk not only about the importance of dummy half running but invariably about marker defence too. They stress the need always to have double markers at the play the ball, working together to ensure both sides are covered, because the space created by the 10-metre rule can give the attacking side very easy gains if marker defence is not up to standard.

Playing the ball efficiently is also reflected in how wisely any side uses its sets of six tackles. A vital component of this is setting

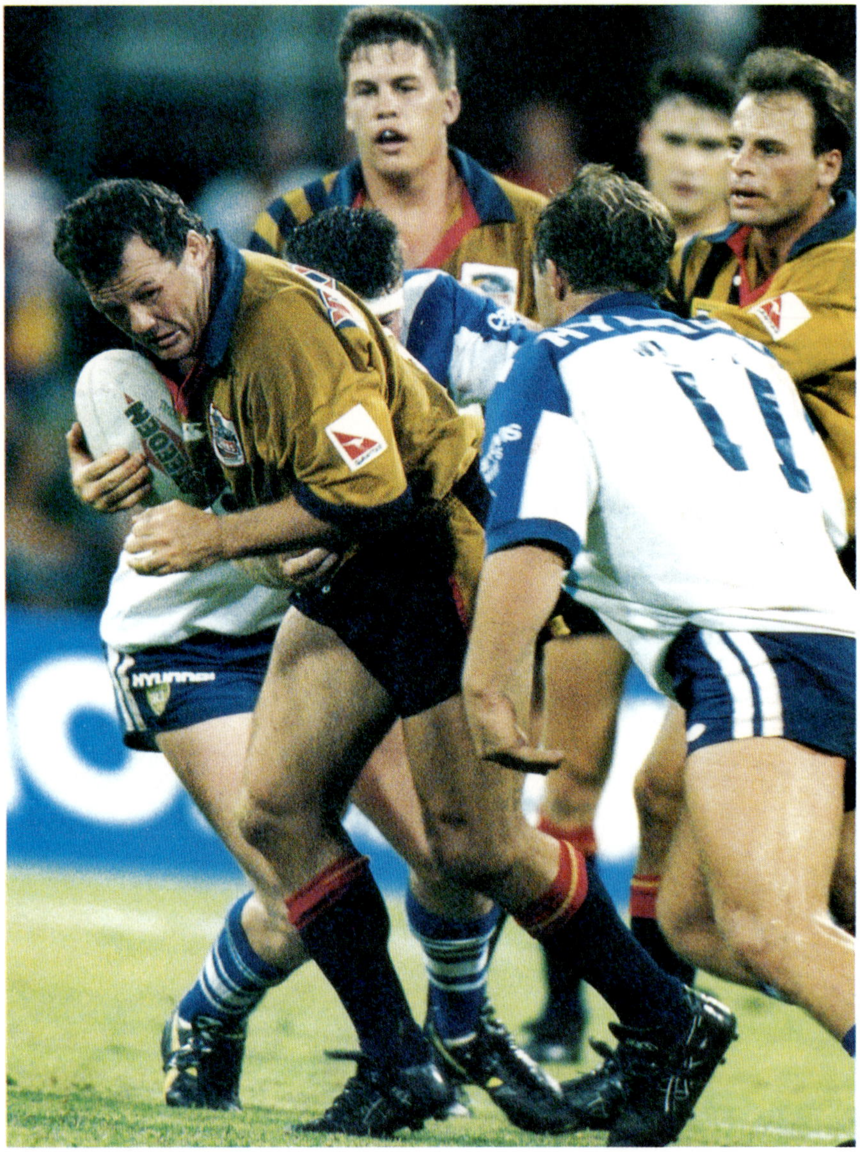

Left: The secret to being able to play the ball quickly is the player's body position when he is tackled. Trevor Gillmeister, who switched from Penrith to Winfield Cup expansion side the South Queensland Crushers in 1995, is seen here, against the Sydney Bulldogs. He is driving forward, leaning over in the tackle, and is in a good position to be able to play the ball quickly when the referee decides the tackle has been completed.

Opposite: One of Mark Geyer's traits is to run tall, so to speak, backing his height to give him the chance of rolling a pass to his supports over the top of tacklers. But the Western Reds second rower isn't faring so well as he is driven back by St George's Jeff Hardy (No 27) and David Barnhill.

up properly on the final tackle for the now-usual kicking option. The nominated kicker — and optional kicker(s) — needs to be stationed correctly, and also requires decent service from the dummy half if he is to put in an effective kick for territory or position, especially from a defensive situation. The slightest hesitation gives the team chasing a chance of closing the kicker down, or hurrying him into a kick which produces minimal or no advantage.

Football teams practise all manner of arts these days but there is little question that a heavy concentration on attacking and defensive options around the play the ball region is central to any team's potential for success. And that is why all players need to be able to play the ball correctly and quickly. By doing that, they help themselves and therefore their team.

PENFOLDS
27
PENFOLDS

PEPSI

THE SCRUM

Scrums today are nowhere near as tightly bound as they used to be, but a class forward still must know all the skills of scrummaging.

Harry Bath (legendary Australian coach)

No single feature in the game of rugby league seems to attract more ridicule than the scrum. Those people who have only a passing interest in league usually label league scrums a joke; even people in the game have a similar attitude.

It is an inescapable fact that league scrums do look like a muddle much of the time, and they don't appeal as an illustration of technical perfection. However, that is a centre's viewpoint, not one the average front rower is likely to agree with. And while league scrums don't look pretty, put in the simplest terms, they are no more than a means of restarting play.

The league scrum engages both sets of forwards, not with the intention of it becoming a test of strength, but with the aim of ensuring the ball is back in play with a minimum of fuss. All six

Opposite: The bowels of a rugby league scrum the way it should look. The openside props have created the channel, enabling the hookers to have a view of the ball when it is thrown in, and the props have their outside legs poised to strike for the ball.

Right: Scrum ball, if it emerges quickly, provides one of the best openings for a team to try a shock move on the first tackle. In this case, Manly halfback Geoff Toovey immediately feeds his backline from a scrum while his loose forward Owen Cunningham has broken to provide some protection from any fast-breaking Brisbane players.

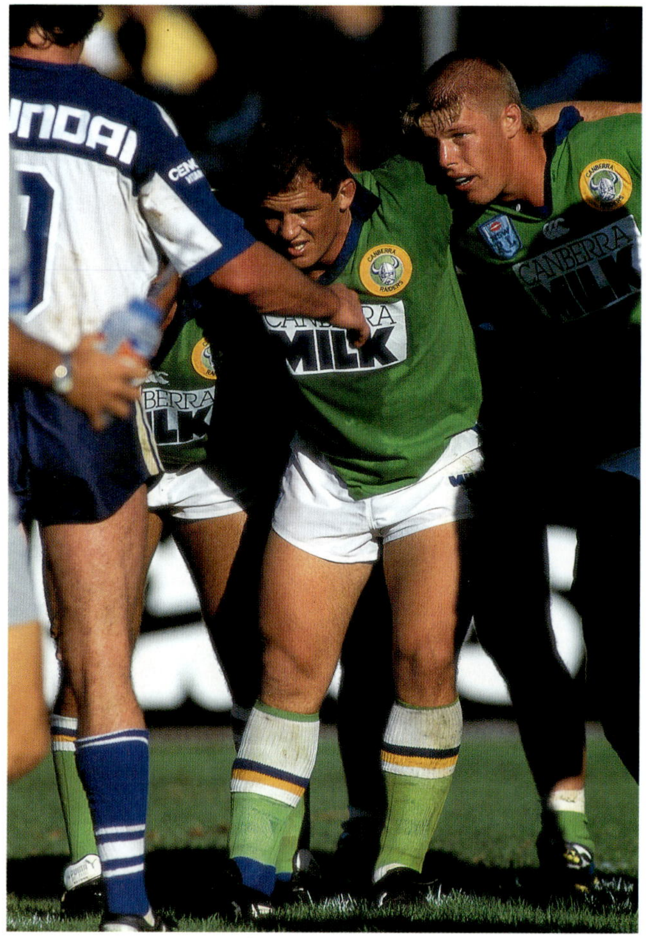

forwards must be involved, or bound, when a scrum is put down. The front row comprises two props and a hooker. The openside prop packs down on the side of the scrum from which the halfback is putting the ball in; the blindside prop does the same on the furthest side of the scrum, and the hooker packs down in between them. The two second rowers pack down behind the front row and the loose forward in behind and between the second rowers.

League scrums are not generally noted for their drive and cohesion because there is no great premium placed on these attributes. Scrums can look like six players making up the numbers, standing up to the opposition and, once the ball is cleared, breaking off to get into the attacking or defensive line. But perhaps more attention should be directed towards scrummaging; improved technique and creating an attitude where a team actually attempts to push the opposition off their scrum ball. It could be a more than useful shock tactic as most sides don't expect it to happen.

Above left: The front row view, with one of the game's greatest hookers the focus of attention. Lodged between his props, Balmain's now-retired Benny Elias hoists himself up for another scrum.

Above: Canberra's front row about to pack against their Canterbury-Bankstown counterparts. Hooker Steve Walters has his arms bound over the shoulders of his props Brett Hetherington and John Lomax (obscured), so he can hang off them and strike for the ball.

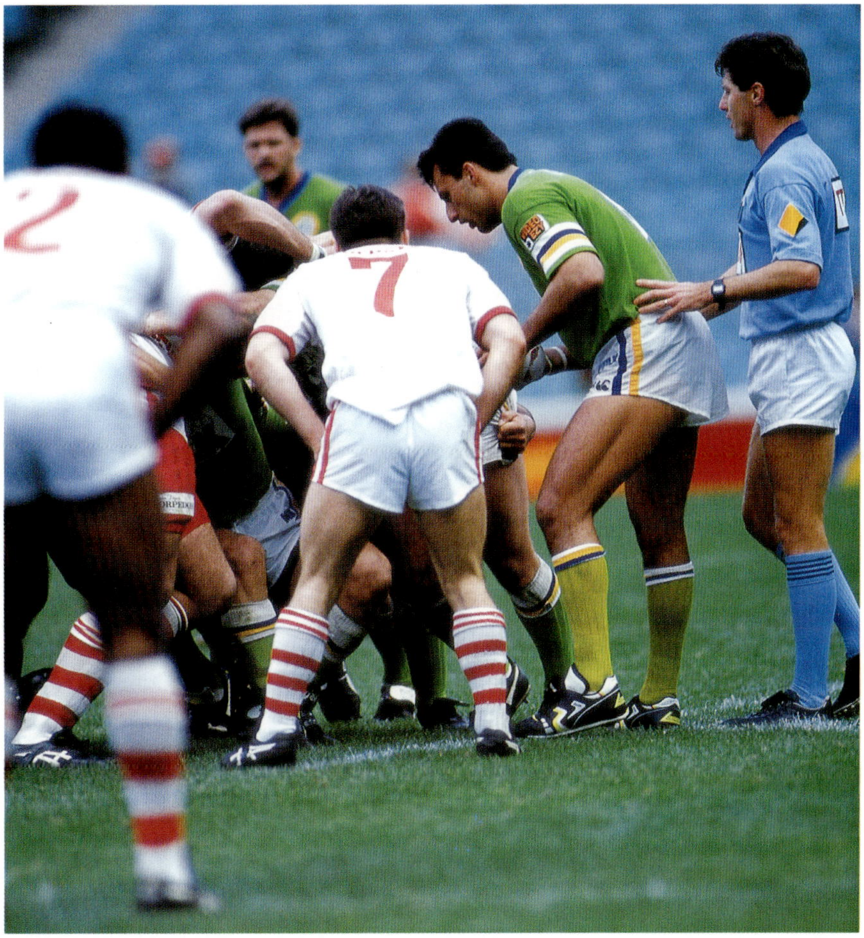

Right: Referee Bill Harrigan hovers as Laurie Daley prepares to feed Canberra's scrum. Inside the tunnel it is possible to make out Steve Walters positioning himself as advantageously as possible so he can hook the ball back.

When I started playing first grade league as a teenager for the Manukau Club in Auckland, putting my head into a scrum wasn't in my plans. I had always wanted to be a centre or winger. Essentially, it has stayed that way throughout my league career, although in my years at Wigan I did play in the No 13 jersey quite a few times and so had to savour the dubious delights of scrummaging. When I was picked to play loose forward, taping the ears down was a priority; I wasn't about to develop those cauliflower jobs.

Because of its perceived lack of importance, any number of illegalities during scrums could be picked up by a referee, including incorrect binding; the hooker dropping the loose arm; striking too early for the ball; the non-feeding halfback not retiring, and many more. And it is rare to see a scrum these days where a halfback is not technically in breach of the rules when feeding the ball. So many times, the ball will be fed in via the second row rather than the so-called 'correct channel' — between the two front rows. Referees tend to adopt a realistic attitude and allow the same infringements for both sides, except in extreme cases. The argument is why pick on petty infringements, which only slow the game down, when the idea of the scrum is basically for the non-offending team to gain possession?

The downside of this is that the old-fashioned hooker, the true striker, has more or less been driven out of the game at the highest level, and there are now very few instances of hookers winning the ball against the head. This used to be commonplace and hookers prided themselves in checking the statistics to find out how many scrums they had taken against the feed.

These days, Winfield Cup teams can be found using converted halfbacks at hooker. The most obvious example is Mark Soden at North Sydney; he's become a permanent fixture in the Bears' No 9 jersey. Des Hasler has also played at hooker for Manly and, when Bobby Goulding was at Wigan, the team went through a phase when he was used as hooker. While they may be small men, they have great speed with which to make darts from dummy half — Soden, in particular, makes a lot of ground for Norths that way — as well as smart ball distribution skills.

Opposite: Scrums can test a referee's patience more than any other facet of the game. The problem for them is getting the front rows to pack correctly; that often means lecturing the players before the ball can be fed in.

There are critics who believe the scrum should be abolished in league; their complaint is not so much founded on the shambles that scrums can become, but more on the fact that scrums slow the game down. Without them, they say, the ball would be in play more. That would certainly be the case, but it is not hard to imagine that there are more than a few players who welcome the odd scrum to give them a breather and the chance to re-focus.

Efforts have been made through the years to restrict the number of scrums. The introduction of the hand-over was the most obvious. Until then, being caught in possession on the sixth tackle meant a scrum; so did kicking the ball out on the full on the last tackle. Do that on the final tackle now and it is an automatic hand-over.

With these sorts of changes, scrums are hardly a dominant feature of the game and they occur for relatively few offences. Among them are knock-ons, forward passes, an attacking player held up in goal, the ball carrier being taken into touch, the ball being passed into touch (when missing the intended target) and a kick in general play being put into touch.

The suggestion has been made that rather than a scrum, play could resume with the non-offending team being given the ball; just like a hand-over when caught in possession on the final tackle, and there may be merit in this. It is not unusual to see games when the number of scrums is in single figures; when Australia and Great Britain clashed in the second test of the

TNT
TDK

Ashes series in 1994, the scrum count was just 4–2 in Australia's favour. And in the Canberra versus Canterbury-Bankstown Winfield Cup grand final in 1994 there were only 10 scrums in total.

The scrum may not be prevalent in rugby league, but it remains a vital basis for launching an attack. While the basic philosophy is to use your full complement of six tackles to create a try-scoring chance, the scrum often provides one of the best openings to strike instantly. With the modern-day trend of putting the fullback right up in the defensive line for scrums, there is a huge invitation to chip the ball over the top on the first tackle; if you've got a Martin Offiah in your backline,

Above: The most common option from a scrum, provided the ball has emerged quickly and cleanly, is for the halfback, in this case North Sydney's Jason Taylor, to feed the ball to his first receiver.

Above right: Canterbury-Bankstown's Kevin Moore gets the desired result from a scrum feed against Canberra. The word 'desired' could almost be replaced by 'automatic' because these days there are very few scrums won against the feed.

wouldn't you? And increasingly you see sides trying to lay on a try-scoring option on an early tackle from a scrum in the opposition's 20-metre zone.

As a set piece, the scrum is an ideal time to orchestrate your attack. Going for the four-pointer on the first tackle, or very early in the tackle count, doesn't always produce a try, but some sides have a high success rate, especially in England where defences aren't always what they could be in some of the inferior sides.

It happens at test level, too. Perhaps one of the very best examples of a set play from the scrum was in only the second test I played for New

Zealand. It was Lang Park, Brisbane, the second test against Australia in 1983. We'd conceded an early try but were awarded a scrum not far from the Aussies' line.

Leading up to the test, Graham Lowe had worked out a move on the blackboard designed for just this situation. Australia's three key players around the scrum base were Ray Price at loose forward, Steve Mortimer at halfback and Wally Lewis at stand-off, and Graham wanted a way of committing all three on defence from an attacking scrum.

He explained it best in his biography Lowe and Behold*:*
"We swapped Nicky Wright from fullback to stand-off, Gordon Smith from stand-off to loose forward and Gary Prohm from

Left: One of the options from the scrum — Illawarra loose forward Ian Russell picks the ball up off the back of the scrum and has a scamper himself.

Preceding pages: The ball has arrived sweetly from the scrum and Canterbury-Bankstown halfback Craig Polla-Mounter is able to move it to his backline well before his Canberra opposite Trevor Schodel can get anywhere near him.

loose forward to fullback. I felt Nicky had more ability to beat a man from a standing start than anyone else in the team and Gary had the strength coming on to the ball to require at least one more player close to the line to handle him. We gambled on Wally Lewis having a handful handling Nicky which would require Mortimer to be involved in the tackle in that play and, when Price saw Gary coming through after getting the ball from Nicky, he'd have to be involved in the defensive play as well. As long as we had a quick play the ball from Gary we'd have the three key Aussies committed and all we'd have to do would be to peel one of our second rowers from the scrum, have him running one off the pivot and we should have an overlap —

Right: A master at grabbing any chance from a scrum, Canberra's Ricky Stuart is focussed on securing the ball. But from there he has so many options: he might connect with a runner hitting a shorter pass; he could fling a long ball to his stand-off, or maybe an even longer one out to the centres; or he could sneak away for a run down the shortside and link up with his winger or a forward breaking from the scrum on his inside.

and that's exactly what happened. Fred Ah Kuoi got the ball quickly when Gary played the ball, with those three Aussie players committed, and he put Westy (Graeme West) over without a hand on him."

To pull a move directly from a scrum like that was just the ultimate; to do so in a test against Australia, well, that was quite sensational. That move and the resulting try perfectly illustrates what can be worked from the scrum, especially these days when you are virtually guaranteed of winning your own feed (not the case in 1983).

In certain instances the scrum is a tailor-made platform from which to attack and there can be any number of variations. The blindside winger can be dragged in as an extra man or decoy runner, or the fullback can be used the same way. Or there is the seemingly fundamental but successful ploy of the loose forward, halfback and winger combining down the short side. The Warriors worked it beautifully against Illawarra at Ericsson Stadium in 1995. Already leading 32–12, Greg Alexander fed a scrum about 30 metres out from Illawarra's line; loose forward Logan Edwards picked up the ball off the back of the scrum and fed Alexander, who drew the winger and gave Sean Hoppe a free run to the line for a try. Simple, yet so effective.

Trying to score from an early tackle isn't always the best option; often teams will try to work the opposition around from a scrum and set up the try-scoring chance on a later tackle, maybe even on the final one. But to have a shot early — to have a move

Above left: Correct scrum formation. In Newcastle's front row, hooker Robbie McCormack is hanging off the shoulders of his props Mark Sargent (nearest the camera) and Paul Harragon (obscured), while the two second rowers have packed down against the props' rumps. Loose forward Marc Glanville is poised to pack in between his two second rowers.

Above: St George halfback Noel Goldthorpe observes the basics at scrum time against

Canterbury-Bankstown. With referee Greg McCallum watching, Goldthorpe follows the ball through the scrum. Notice also how the Canterbury loose forward is still bound to the scrum, as he should be.

Following pages: Canterbury-Bankstown and Illawarra at scrum time. Illawarra loose forward John Cross is about to pack in at the back of the scrum and referee Greg McCallum warns the Bulldogs' defensive line to stay on-side.

designed to do that — can have tremendous value as a shock tactic. You just have to pick the right time.

While league scrums can be a bit untidy, it is what the scrum can provide for a team that matters. For the attacking side, the alternatives are limitless; and for teams on deep defence a scrum can be a godsend as well. Perhaps an opposition attack has broken down with a forward pass or knock on just metres from the goal line, resulting in a scrum; it is a valuable break for a defending side that has just been busted as it provides a chance to slow play down and allows the defence to regroup before battling out of the defensive zone. As long as the scrum is part of league, it is a facet of the game which should be used, not abused.

BHP

the best.

PENALTIES

Discipline is like a health diet. We may not care for it ourselves but know it is good for everybody else.

Jack Gibson (legendary Australian coach)

A rugby league match is generally at its best when scrums are at a minimum. That usually translates to a game which has been spared too many errors and has been able to flow. The same applies to penalties; the fewer there are in a match, the better it will be as a spectacle. In the same way as scrums, penalties often number less than 10 a match and not commonly 20 or more. Obviously the number is dependent on key factors like playing conditions, the referee in charge and the players' attitudes to discipline. But when those ingredients are equal, the spread in penalty counts can total as few as half a dozen a game.

The game from hell is one which has 20 or more scrums and an equal ration of penalties. To have 40-odd stoppages for errors and infringements does not make for a wonderful match to watch, nor is it great to play in. Fortunately this situation is uncommon when teams of high quality clash. Players at this

Opposite: Take the two! A cry that often goes up when a penalty is awarded near the posts. And for a side like Canterbury-Bankstown (now the Sydney Bulldogs), with Daryl Halligan's boot to rely on, the go-for-goal option is easy to take.

Right: When kicking for touch from a penalty, there is one rule above all — find touch. Bradford Northern's Deryck Fox has the follow-through right.

Far right: The penalty might be worth only two points, but its value should not be under-estimated. Hull's Paul Eastwood tries to make it count.

level are able to minimise mistakes and don't care too much for testing the referee's patience or interpretation of the rules.

In England in the last season or two, the incidence of penalties has probably tended towards a slightly higher level as referees crack down on certain aspects of the game. They have taken a tough line on high tackles, with even tackles which don't seem close to borderline resulting in penalties (or sin binnings and dismissals). They are also policing the play the ball area more strictly.

It is the high or dangerous tackle which contributes significantly to the penalty count in most games. Referees are also intent, at least early in a match, on ensuring the defensive side observes the 10-metre rule. Other acts that will incur penalties include:

- the deliberate forward pass
- being off side chasing a kick
- holding down the tackled player too long
- tackling a player when not in possession
- running obstruction, using a fellow player as a shepherd (a team-mate without the ball who deliberately obstructs a would-be tackler)
- a variety of play the ball offences and illegalities surrounding the scrum

Opposite: The high tackle — the provider of a fair proportion of penalties in rugby league matches. The nature of the game means they are unavoidable to a degree because of the need to effect tackles which wrap up both the ball and the man. But this is of no consequence to the referee — it is an offence which will lead to a penalty (not to mention a possible sin binning or an ordering off).

Foul play in its various shapes — punching or kicking an opponent, use of the elbow, forearm, knees and so on — along with abuse of the referee and dissent will be penalised.

But you do find at the highest level there is a greater respect for the rules. Fighting in any form is now a rarity because most players, and coaches, know the cost is too great. To have a player sin binned or ordered off — and maybe later suspended as well — is a sheer waste, for the team as well as the player.

What is more often seen is the professional foul. A team busted on defence will often feel compelled to do anything they can to prevent a try being scored. If an attack has completely fragmented the defending side, the last defender will deliberately hold down the tackled player. He knows that to let him play the ball will give the opposition a six-point opportunity because his team is hopelessly outnumbered. It is thought better to concede the penalty; giving away two points at the most as compared to six. Referees are trying to curb this practice by putting offenders in the sin bin for 10 minutes which, in this day and age, could ultimately cost their team the game.

Penalties in such cases produce just one logical option for the attacking side. Any team with a Frano Botica, Daryl Halligan,

12

Matthew Ridge or Jason Taylor will go for the two points. A penalty anywhere up to 40 metres out makes that an instinctive and understandable move when a superboot is in the side. Most times, kickers of quality will nail the two points; if they don't, they'll nearly always kick the ball dead in any case, to ensure they get the ball back from the resulting drop-out.

If the decision is to go for the two points, the captain must have confidence — and will expect — that his kicker at least puts the ball dead. That way the decision to go for goal is covered both ways. To kick for goal *and* hand the ball back to the opposition is wasting a set of six tackles.

In deciding whether to go for the shot at goal, the state of the game has to be taken into account. A team hopelessly behind and struggling to gain a fair quota of possession will probably consider passing up the shot at a goal. Just to have a full set of six tackles in possession can often be more valuable in those circumstances but two points on the scoreboard are difficult to ignore.

Just check out what goalkicking has meant for sides like Wigan, Canterbury-Bankstown, North Sydney and Manly-Warringah in recent years. And you can only imagine how many points sides such as Brisbane and Canberra — who haven't been so well off with their kicking percentages — might have scored with a proficient goalkicker.

There are also a lot of indirect penalties awarded in league — essentially for scrum-related infringements. These are indicated by the referee raising his outstretched arm in the penalty gesture and moving it up and down. A shot at goal is not permitted in these cases. However, like the scrum, the penalty still provides a set piece option, and therefore is a great means of mounting an attack. It guarantees possession but in a structured way, immediately creating the chance to use a practised move.

There is a basic rule which simply cannot be reinforced often enough when receiving a penalty. The normal process is to kick the ball into touch, play restarting with a tap kick infield from where the ball went out. If the decision is to go for touch — and most times it is — then it is vital that the designated kicker finds touch. To fail to do so is one of the cardinal sins of the game, and you still see it happen, even at test level, as well as in Winfield Cup and English first division matches.

It is all very well trying to carve off 50 or 60 metres of touchline, but if there is the slightest risk of the ball not going out, then it is wasted effort as it means that the team penalised has immediately been handed the ball and six tackles. Even if the gain is only 15 to 30 metres, it doesn't matter; if the ball goes out every time, you at least have possession further down the field

Above: The tap re-start from a penalty is an ideal time for the team in possession to organise a structured attack. Here Balmain's Benny Elias gives his side instructions on the call before tapping.

Above right: Canterbury-Bankstown's Jarrod McCracken cops 10 minutes in the sin bin for a misdemeanour. This will give the opposition a penalty and a great chance to stretch a side playing one man short.

Following pages: It's a safe bet that a penalty followed this flare-up. Wigan's Shaun Edwards tangles with his former Central Park team-mate, Leeds loose forward Ellery Hanley.

at the tap re-start, and therefore the chance to organise your attack.

A penalty awarded in the middle of the field should be carefully considered. If it is not in range for a shot at goal, then caution should be exercised in deciding whether to put the ball into touch. From that part of the field, the touchline is a fair distance away, more so if the wind is against the kicker. To protect the six tackles you've been handed, the sensible course might be to tap the ball.

From a tap in those circumstances, or from a tap re-start after putting the ball into touch, there are many attacking possibilities. Maybe the idea is simply to go for field position, work the ball as close to the opposition's line as possible, nudge a kick into the in-goal area on a late tackle and look to force a goal-line drop-out (by tackling the ball carrier behind the goal-line or forcing the defending team to put the ball dead). Achieve this and you have the ball back for another six tackles to put even more pressure on the defence. This is percentage play, and is generally highly effective.

If that is not the drill, then there are ample moves off the tap kick which can create try-scoring openings. That is why on the

erg

first tackle the team in possession usually takes the ball a little further in-field — often through one of the wingers — so opening up the shortside and providing plenty of room to attack on either side of the ruck (the play the ball).

There have been plenty of moves from the tap re-start which have worked for teams I've played for over the years, but two of my favourites happened when I played for the Rest of the World against Australia in Sydney in 1988. Graham Lowe coached the side and we must have practised some penalty moves 30 times or more. They worked, though. Kevin Iro scored our first try from a penalty move. But the best one was the second try, which came directly from the tap re-start.

We set up to move the ball on the openside through Andy Gregory and Shane Cooper — but we actually switched the attack to Mark Graham, who had folded around on the shortside and he put Mike Gregory over with ease. It was a great try from a move which worked to absolute perfection. I haven't seen too many to rival it.

Discipline is vital in every sport. In rugby league, teams without it are inviting defeat. The spear tackle is one of the clearest signals that players lack sufficient professional discipline. Here are three tackles which might come into the spear tackle category, qualifying on the basis that the players seem to have lifted the ball carrier unduly, so ensuring he lands head first or on his shoulders. The defending side can only lose in this situation as players involved in obvious or possible spear tackles can expect to be ordered off or at least to be put on report. They will certainly concede a penalty.

Following pages: Goalkicker extraordinaire, Frano Botica. The former All Black became a goalkicking sensation when he switched to league. Always following the same routine has been vital to his success.

The quick tap from a penalty is always an option. To have an Allan Langer or someone as quick as him tap and run when a penalty is awarded can cause real alarm in a defence that hasn't organised itself, or isn't awake to the possibility.

There is also the defensive penalty, which can provide relief for any team that has been under siege inside its 20-metre zone. Like the defensive scrum, it allows a side to slow things down for a few moments and ease the pressure.

Respecting the penalty's value as a direct source of points is important, as is respecting its value as a supplier of possession and, indirectly, the chance to score even more points. Using the penalty as an attacking weapon needs to be thought out clearly and thoroughly. And using it as a means of transforming desperate defence into attack requires just as much thought. There might be very few penalties in some games but the dividend they can yield should always be valued.

MIZUNO

2WS
2WS
asics
asics

TACKLING

There is no greater sensation in rugby league football than the surge of elation, the thrill of conquest, that follows a strong, confidently executed tackle.

Barry Muir (Australian International, 1959–63)

Anyone who has played rugby league should be able to relate to Barry Muir's thoughts on arguably the most crucial facet of the game. If there is a prerequisite to being a successful league player, it is the ability to tackle. That applies to any position on the field. Barry Muir was a halfback; one who owns a place in rugby league's hall of legendary tacklers.

There has always been a fascination in the way the smallest halfbacks bring down the biggest men in the game. Barry Muir was one of them and there have been plenty of others like him since. In the same mould were New Zealand's Ken Stirling and Australian Tom Raudonikis. Later champion tacklers in the Kiwis' No 7 jersey have included Shane Varley, Clayton Friend and Gary Freeman.

Of course, it is not just the small guys who have big reputations as tacklers. Australia has produced most of league's outstanding

Opposite: The ultimate gang tackle, as four Parramatta defenders completely suffocate the Western Suburbs ball carrier. It's a sure-fire way of ensuring the ball is locked up, but by involving so many players in one tackle, it means there must be a weak spot in the defensive line.

Right: It doesn't look too pretty, nor too legal perhaps, but Western Suburbs defenders Darren Willis (left) and Brent Stuart are dealing to Warriors replacement hooker Syd Eru with a double tackle which will stop Eru's progress.

Top and bottom left: Every league season produces its memorable hits. One of the best in 1995 was laid on by Warriors winger Whetu Taewa. The moment his Western Suburbs opposite Brandon Pearson received the ball, Taewa was onto him with the perfect back-slamming tackle. In the top photo, Taewa drives in with his right shoulder. A split second later, Taewa has Smith heading, back first, at a great rate of knots towards the turf.

Opposite: Giant Kangaroo second rower Paul Sironen has nothing else to think about other than the fact that he's going to hit the turf. This is a copy-book up-and-down tackle — one man down low wraps up Sironen's thighs, Great Britain's Chris Joynt clamps on around the shoulders and, as insurance, Barrie McDermott is ready to pitch in from the left.

tacklers and many of them have been forwards. Right now you could roll out a staggering list of them from Winfield Cup sides, including Bradley Clyde, David Gillespie, Ian Roberts, Paul Harragon, David Fairleigh, Gary Larson, Mark Carroll, Trevor Gillmeister, Peter Johnston and Danny Lee. And, in no time, Hitro Okesene built the same reputation for the Warriors in 1995. Most of these players also hurt in the tackle, although the likes of Larson and Lee are known more for their high output than for the impact and damage factor of their defence.

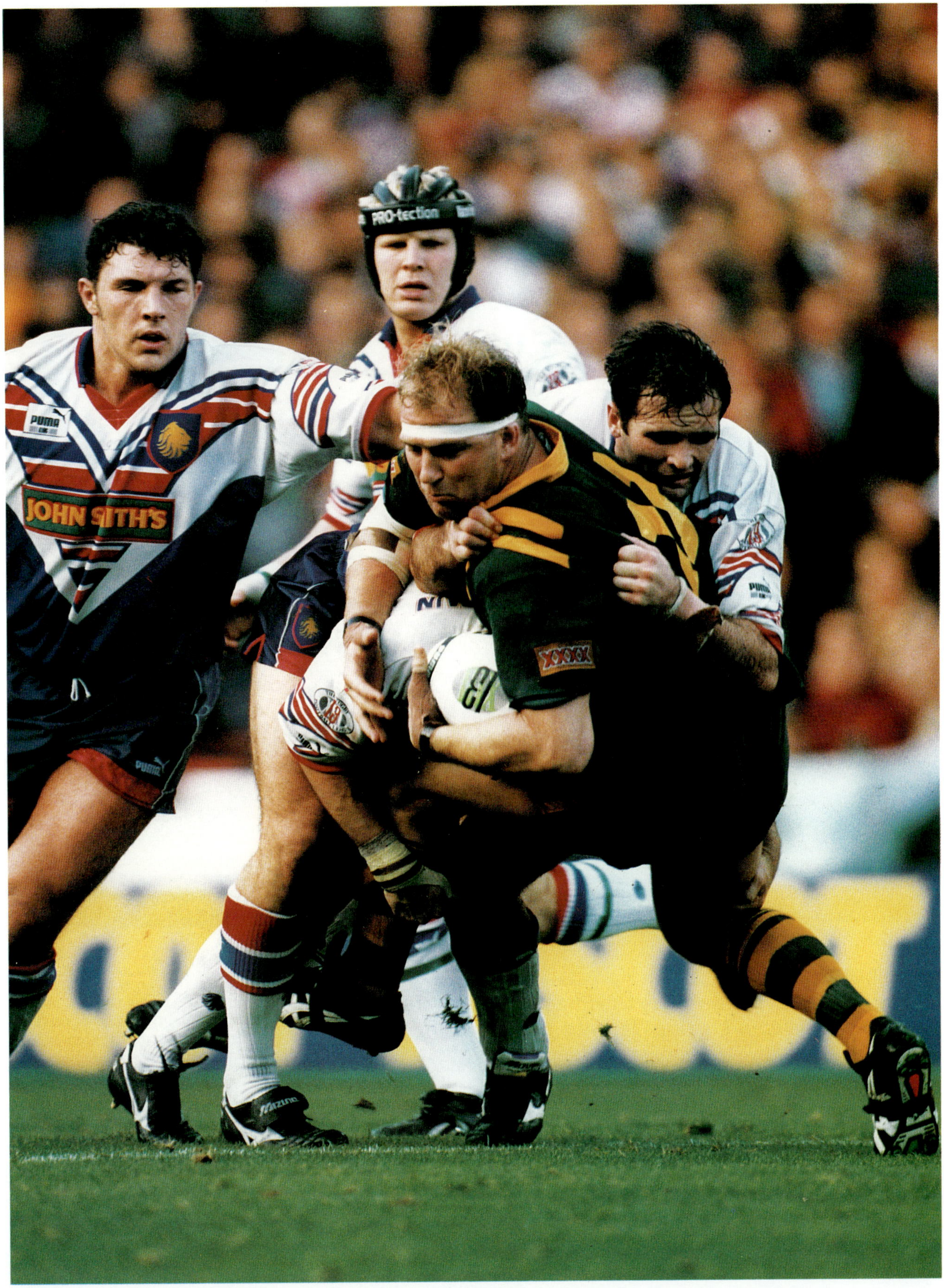
PRO-tection
PUMA
XXXX

Above: Wigan second rower Denis Betts is airborne and sandwiched as Warrington's Kelly Shelford wraps up the man and the ball high, while hooker Tukere Barlow goes low.

Tackling standards have improved markedly in England since the mid 1980s, and certainly tackling became one of the strongest facets of Wigan's game. It used to be said, especially by Australians, that the game in Britain paid little or no attention to defence; that couldn't be said now. Although perhaps it is fair to say that the defensive aspect of the Australian game is still more demanding and efficient, coaches quite rightly placing a high premium on their defence. Jack Gibson has said: "The fact is, if your defence is good you're never going to get beat." A real Gibsonism that one — and so true.

Above right: Among league's smaller players, Manly's Geoff Toovey is one of the biggest tacklers. Robust South Sydney prop Terry Hermansson looks well-braced to bump Toovey off in a 1994 Winfield Cup clash, but Toovey, so adept at timing his drive into a tackle, doesn't often 'lose out' in confrontations like this.

Defence isn't merely tackling on its own, of course; it is all about having the right defensive organisation, about positional play and having a defensive line which operates in unison. The aspects of defence are addressed in a later chapter, for now the focus is on just one element of defence, the tackle itself.

It can be an utterly thankless task making tackle after tackle. The tackling addicts like, say, Cronulla prop Danny Lee and North Sydney second rower Gary Larson, are credited with an amazing number of tackles almost every week. Sometimes they might be as high as 45 or more in one match (although the business of judging what constitutes a tackle is strongly debated by some people). But officially in 1994, Lee topped 800 tackles in Cronulla's Winfield Cup matches, an average of more than 36 a game! All teams at top level can do with a forward with that sort of work rate in defence.

The game's tackling machines aren't always readily or regularly noticed and appreciated. Ray Price was an exception and, over a period of years, he deservedly gained the tag 'Perpetual Motion'. That was because at almost every moment of any game, Price seemed to be involved either making a tackle, taking the ball up or backing up.

The tacklers who are best remembered are those who have a habit of leaving their calling card; and their calling card is usually pain. For many years, David 'Cement' Gillespie was the most feared tackler in the Winfield Cup — just watching him at work was painful enough — and Ian Roberts has been known to be just as damaging when 'spotting' a player.

Right: Making the tackle is one thing, completing it is another. Kiwi captain Gary Freeman has decked Great Britain's Jonathan Davies but wants to add a little 'finish' to the tackle.

Left: It's not usually advised that a smaller player goes high on a big one. And the equation of Penrith centre Matt Sing tangling with massive Illawarra prop Darren Fritz wouldn't normally add up, but in this instance Fritz has already been taken low, his momentum checked, and Sing is finishing off over the top.

Far left: Being 'monstered' in defence takes on special meaning when it's giant Kiwi centre Kevin Iro smothering Great Britain winger Jason Robinson.

For sheer impact, total commitment and ferocity one tackle is constantly remembered by New Zealanders and, I'm sure, by Australians too. Mention the name Kevin Tamati and the answer should be instant; his amazing hit on Australian forward Rohan Hancock early in the first test at Lang Park in 1982. It just flattened Hancock.

Apart from big hits like that, the tackles never forgotten are those that have saved tries, or let tries in. One in each of those categories comes to mind from my test days.

For a try-saver, you'd need some imagination to better the effort Nick Wright produced in the second test against Australia in 1983. That was the one the Kiwis won 19–12, but not before Wright's sensational sideline tackle on a try-bound Mal Meninga.

There didn't seem to be any chance of Meninga being stopped but, in a blur of arms and legs, Nicky stunned him by bowling him into touch just metres from the corner flag. Brilliant. It inspired the rest of us.

Two years later, it was the opposite at the same ground. Not so much a case of a tackle missed as such, more a case of poor positioning in defence. It was the first test of the 1985 series, the score locked at 20–all with less than 10 minutes to go. The Australians moved the ball to the left side of the field, Wally Lewis flicking out one of his special long passes to create enough room for John Ribot to score the winner.

I've always felt I was badly positioned in defence when that try was scored and was at least partly to blame. As it happened, Ribot also scored a late match-winner in the second test in Auckland, so costing us the chance of a series win.

RL

Opposite: A welcome to tackling in the big league for former All Black John Timu. Switching to league for the 1995 Winfield Cup season, the Sydney Bulldogs signing immediately found himself the target of extra attention on defence.

Right: Illawarra's tacklers have picked up Warriors prop Hitro Okesene, but his momentum hasn't been halted. It takes extreme power in a head-on situation for tacklers to stop Okesene dead.

There are so many keys to being an effective tackler. Good positioning is important, so is self-confidence in being able to make a tackle; the moment you lack confidence you are in strife. Naturally, strength, as distinct from size, is a requirement as well. Attitude, so important in every phase of the game, is absolutely vital in the art of tackling. You need to be mentally, as well as physically, prepared to tackle, your body and mind tensed to make impact. Another vital element in tackling is moving up quickly on defence — never sit back and wait, commit yourself fully.

The low tackle

If you're making a low tackle, set yourself to hit the man just above the knees and focus your eyes on that target, not on the ball carrier's eyes. Watch his legs and you will know where he is heading. Drive your shoulder — and it pays to work hard on being able to tackle with either shoulder instead of favouring

one — hard into the target; if you are less than forceful, the tackle will be ineffective. Once you've hit the spot, clench your arms around the ball carrier's legs, yanking them together with a real snap. Keep your head behind his thighs to ensure it doesn't get sandwiched between his legs and the ground, possibly causing injury. And always hold on until the referee rules the ball carrier held.

Head-on tackle

Of course, different types of tackles require slightly different techniques. Always you'll hear that the head-on tackle is the most difficult one to make, and it is a type of tackle that needs to be made regularly. And simply effecting a tackle isn't all that matters, you must also ensure that the ball carrier isn't able to off-load the ball. This applies especially to the head-on tackle.

In league, there aren't too many sights better than a perfectly executed head-on ball-and-all tackle. It is all about timing. Mark Graham was a master of it in his playing days. You need to rush up on an opponent and hit him soon after he receives the ball; before he has any time to organise himself. That is the secret.

The ankle tackle can be highly effective, but it can also be highly hazardous to the tackler. The difficulty is clamping on and sticking to the ball carrier's ankles long enough to bring him down.

Above left: Wigan winger Jason Robinson easily steps out of a would-be low tackle to scamper away.

Above: The ankle tackle fails again. Australian prop Glenn Lazarus can't hang on to strong-running Great Britain centre Paul Newlove.

A player of average or above average size should have the strength to effect the one-on-one tackle which also wraps up the ball, provided he abides by the number one rule of driving in hard at the target with his shoulder. Arm tackles won't work going high on a ball carrier who has some pace on.

Small players can't usually afford to hit the ball carrier too high in a head-on confrontation, although Manly's Geoff Toovey consistently disproves that theory. Generally, the small player is better advised to go *with* the ball carrier in such a tackle. Instead of trying to drive in, let the big man come to you, aim just below the knees, keeping your head to one side so you don't get hit, and then clench your arms firmly around his legs. Stick to him, and his forward momentum will bring him down.

Right: It's unorthodox, but the aim of the tackle has been achieved. The tackle has lowered the ball carrier, literally ball and all.

JOHN S
PUMA

Opposite: This is the everything-goes style of tackle. Australian prop Paul Harragon literally takes a grab of anything he can on Great Britain front rower Karl Harrison. The jersey gets a quality control test from Harragon's yank with his left arm, while Harrison's unmentionables are in greater danger downunder. It's sometimes referred to as the Christmas hold.

Right: Kiwi second rower Stephen Kearney gets the up-and-under treatment in the tackle from St George in his Western Suburbs days.

Smother tackle (ball-and-all)

The smother tackle is well-named — it is also known as the ball-and-all tackle. The head-on tackle mentioned above is often executed lower down and will not necessarily lock up the ball. As he is about to go down, the ball carrier can still free the ball to support players. League players need to be able to handle the all-engulfing tackle where you wrap your arms around the ball carrier's arms, ensuring he doesn't free the ball. Again this tackle is all about using your strength and driving in as hard as possible.

Double teaming in the tackle will generally succeed on all counts. One player can go low to bring the ball carrier down, the other goes higher to envelop the arms and the ball.

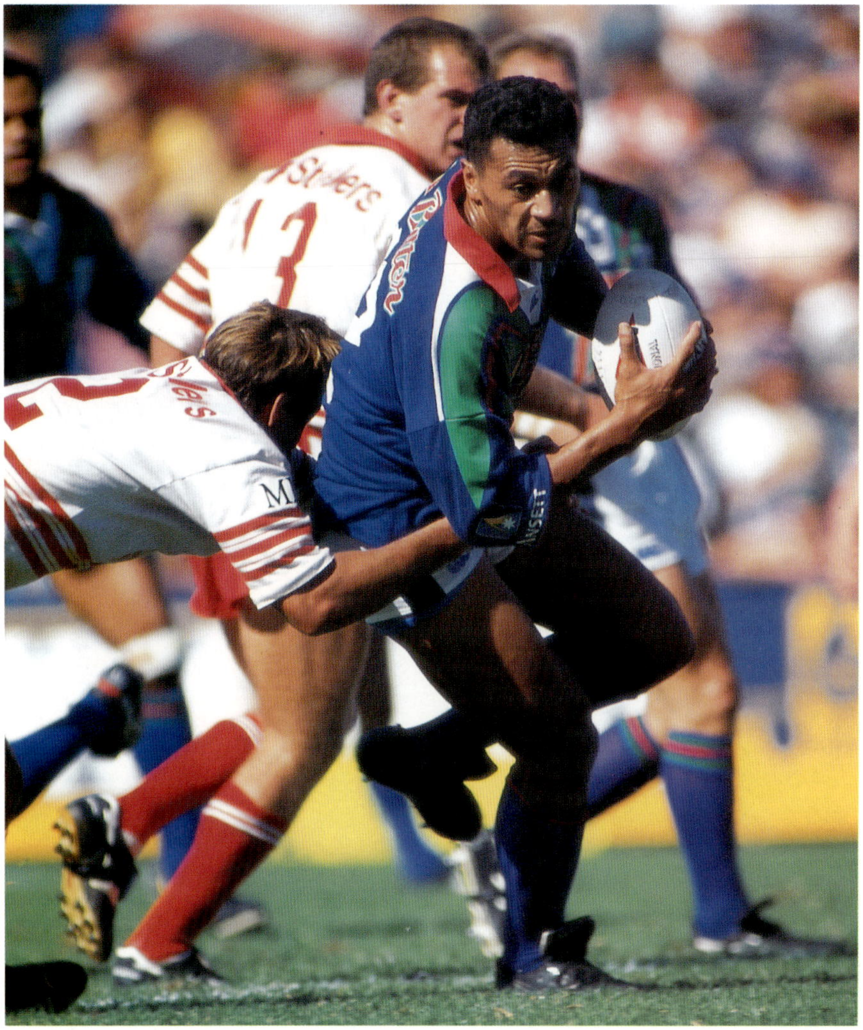

Left: Illawarra winger Rod Wishart has a hold on Warriors second rower Tony Tatupu, but that's all. The tackle really is next to no use because Tatupu hasn't been bothered by a second tackler, leaving his arms and the ball free to pick up a support player.

Opposite top: This has the look of being close to an illegal tackle. Great Britain's Jason Robinson has been picked up by Australia's Glenn Lazarus with some help from Bradley Clyde. If Robinson was tipped any further and driven into the ground shoulders or head first, it would constitute a spear tackle.

Opposite bottom left and right: The Welsh throw everything at Australian winger Wendell Sailor in their 1994 clash, including a swinging arm at the head.

The tackle from behind

The tackle from behind is also an important one to work on, as long as you have the pace to catch the man in possession. You can drive yourself at the attacking player's legs from behind and bring him down with telling effect. Going a little higher will be just as effective as long as you are able to avoid or negate his fend.

Goal-line tackle

Tackling close to your own goal-line is the most demanding. To go low in that situation serves little use; the ball carrier will be able to drive over the top and still dot the ball down. Here, you must be able to execute a full-on body tackle, aimed around the chest so you knock the attacking player backwards, or, at worst, prevent him making any forward progress.

Left: A poor tackle is in the making here. Because Warriors stand-off Gene Ngamu has all but run around him, Western Suburbs fullback Andrew Leeds is left grasping desperately to get some sort of hold.

Opposite: Canterbury-Bankstown's defence has failed. Jason Lowrie has carted the ball up for Eastern Suburbs, found the tackling soft, and been able to stand and deliver.

Following pages: Not classic defence but still effective and, at the end of the day, that's what matters most in tackling. The idea is to stop the ball carrier and prevent him moving the ball. Somehow these two Wigan players have done that to a Bradford Northern player in the English first division. They earn points for effect, none for style or grace.

Side-on tackle

Much easier is the side-on tackle, especially when you have been able to position the ball carrier towards the touchline. As long as he can't beat you for pace, then you have him perfectly set up; drive in with the shoulder around thigh level, or around his rib cage if you want to prevent him passing the ball to any players backing up infield. Be sure your head is positioned behind the player you are tackling.

High tackle

Rugby league does lend itself to the high tackle, sometimes too high, and referees have worked to eliminate this from the game worldwide. High is above the shoulders, but anything below is fair game and there are few more effective, and painful, tackles than the ones which pummel the ball carrier around chest level, or better still, drive up into the rib cage. Those are the David Gillespie specials.

But with all tackles, the same points emerge. The qualities needed are attitude (in terms of courage and confidence), timing, technique, concentration and basic strength. And never have an in-built fear of getting hurt when making a tackle; any hint of fear and you have every chance of being injured. It is also an aspect of rugby league which requires the utmost dedication at training. If you can, practise against live targets; at worst keep hitting those tackle bags.

NORWEB

PEPSI SEA

KICKING

I'm kicking 100 per cent better than when I was playing (rugby union) for North Harbour, but I hardly practised then. I do now because it's my job. It helps me to get a contract.

Frano Botica (All Black and Kiwi International)

Kicking in its different forms was all but ignored in rugby league not too many years ago. There was little attention paid to the importance of goalkicking and, certainly in some countries, there wasn't too much tactical kicking done. This was the case even at test level.

Opposite: Matthew Ridge has been an outstanding success as a fullback for Manly and the Kiwis, giving both sides a potent all-around kicking game and some of the highest-quality goalkicking anyone could hope to see.

Dennis Williams used to have a fair kicking game, but I know when I started playing for the Kiwis the kicking side of the game was fairly new. Graham Lowe had to work to find players who could handle the responsibility. Gary Kemble was probably the player used most regularly to kick for field position and for the line. Darrell Williams was another, as was Hugh McGahan. We weren't big on kicking, and certainly I wasn't a consideration — kicking has never been one of my fortés!

The goal kicking side wasn't much of an improvement. Though there were exceptions in Australia, like Mick Cronin and Michael O'Connor,

Right: It's a routine Daryl Halligan's followed thousands of times: eyes down and watching his target spot on the ball; arms out to provide balance on the approach; his kicking leg cocked back and ready to fire through the ball; his non-kicking foot landing in the preferred area to the left of the ball.

and Balmain had a decent kicker from long range in Ross Conlon. In those days, Mal Meninga was a fair goalkicker (which might surprise a few people given his success later in his career), but the Kiwis were always short on a high-quality goalkicker.

However, players like Australian Wally Lewis had much to do with the kicking revolution which has been so much a part of rugby league in the '90s, at least in the southern hemisphere. Today, you don't have a rugby league team if you don't have a kicking game; it is crucial to success.

If Lewis generated a real awareness about the value of kicking in general play, then the influx of rugby union players was also a major contributing factor, especially on the goalkicking front. Jonathan Davies had a huge impact when he signed for Widnes, both with his goalkicking and his general kicking (and he's still doing the same for Warrington).

But the face of rugby league changed even more with the arrival of the various New Zealand rugby union players — starting with Matthew Ridge in 1990 and then through John Gallagher, John Schuster, Frano Botica, Daryl Halligan, Gavin Hill and Eion Crossan. At one time or another they have all been exceptionally useful as points-scorers. In Ridge, Botica and Halligan, New Zealand has given rugby league arguably the world's three best goalkickers; they have been quite astonishing with their prolific scoring ability and also their level of accuracy.

Frano was just amazing for us at Wigan. I guess in the end he stopped surprising us because we expected him to land every attempt he took, even if he had five in a row from either sideline. The only surprise was when he actually missed one. As a kicker in his rugby union days, Frano says his success rate was never anything too special at all, only because he didn't practise. I know he practised at Wigan. When he wasn't having some shots at training, he'd even roll up a sock and use it as a tee so he could practise in the street outside his place in Wigan. It all worked for him and his kicking certainly won plenty of games for us.

The real value of great goalkickers is that they are demoralising for the opposition, as they virtually ensure the score increases by six points every time a try is scored. Those extra two points not only help on the scoreboard, but also affect the opposition's confidence.

An indication of the importance of the kicker is that in the Winfield Cup, Halligan was the competition's top points scorer in each of his first four seasons playing league, three times with North Sydney and in 1994 with Canterbury-Bankstown (now

Many rugby league players have carefully honed their kicking skills in recent times, one of the game's premier exponents being North Sydney halfback Jason Taylor. He is competent in all facets of kicking, and here, going for territory, is a study of intense concentration.

the Sydney Bulldogs), and Ridge has been right up with the pace in his first five seasons at Manly (apart from 1993 when he had injury problems).

Until players of this quality came along, league kickers had often been toe kickers, with Conlon and O'Connor among the exceptions with their round the corner styles. But when the New Zealanders arrived it was round the corner style for just about everyone.

Even though each kicker has his own little habits, there are basic steps to follow. Placing the ball correctly is vital. It needs to be placed upright, and might even be leaning forward, which

is what legendary rugby union All Black Grant Fox always did. The kicker's contact point is a spot about two centimetres up from the bottom of the ball on the side facing him. The ball's seam should be directly in line with the posts and must be standing upright, not leaning to one side.

To organise his run-up, a kicker should stand over the ball, placing his kicking foot directly behind the ball, his non-kicking one in line with the goalposts and a small distance — a hip's width — from and alongside the ball.

The run-up can be measured in various ways. Some kickers simply turn around and walk back to a spot they think will work, and then turn again to face the ball. Most step back their desired number of steps, then across two steps or so to give them an arced run to the ball. Some step back in an arced fashion from the start. It's really a personal choice; whatever suits the individual.

Once at the top of the mark, the crucial factor now is to focus on the ball, and on the intended contact point. Most kickers indulge in breathing routines to ready themselves before

The influx of rugby union players has had much to do with the improvements in kicking in rugby league. More than a few of them have come from Welsh rugby, like Jonathan Davies and Jonathan Griffiths. Playing for Great Britain against Australia, Davies (above left) is well-positioned for the downtown kick. Like Davies, Jonathan Griffiths (above right) has injected kicking expertise into league. He is captured here on the follow-through as he kicks for territory.

Above: When defenders are swarming in for a charge-down, it is not always possible to launch into a full-blown downfield kick. The Warriors' former Australian test halfback Greg Alexander seems to be stabbing at the ball, rather than operating at full-stretch.

Above right: It is a fair bet that the halfback, stand-off and fullback will be the principal figures in any team's kicking game. But it helps if the hooker is also a capable kicker. As a left footer, Jim Serdaris gives Western Suburbs yet another option.

beginning their approach. What must happen with the run-up is that the non-striking foot must be planted a hip's width from the ball, as it was when preparing for the kick. This should enable the kicker's shoulders to come forward with his head over the ball.

The kicking leg should then be able to strike the ball at the bottom of its swing and, as long as there's a good follow-through, the ball should have a fair chance of producing two points (allowing that it also depends on conditions underfoot, the weather, nerves and the like).

Drop goal (field goal)

While the drop goal, or field goal, is worth only one point in rugby league, its value can be immense. If you are leading a game by six, 12 or 18 points, the one-pointer is the perfect way to provide a comfort zone, stretching it to seven, 13 or 19. Then its value can be seen. And as a tie-breaker in a game which is locked up, the field goal is just priceless. There is a point to remember, though. A field goal attempt cannot be touched in

Traveland.
NSW
RL
STEEDEN
INTERNATIONAL

Opposite: Brisbane's Allan Langer doesn't have the same distance and accuracy in his long kicking game as Ricky Stuart, but the Australian halfback is exceptionally dangerous with the variety and potency of his short kicks — grubbers to the in-goal area, bombs, crossfield kicks for wingers and chip kicks.

Right: Ricky Stuart is the king of many talents on the rugby league field, and he has refined the passing and kicking aspects of the game into the finest of arts. State of Origin time for New South Wales and he belts one of his massive punts downfield, probably a metre off the ground in the process.

flight to be ruled successful, which is why opposition players make such desperate efforts to get a hand on an attempt.

It is also a more difficult kick to master. The kicker generally needs to be balanced to succeed, dropping the ball upright around six or seven centimetres in front of his kicking foot. The technique involved to connect effectively might be likened to catching a cricket ball on the half volley (in other words collecting it just an instant after it has touched the ground). With the field goal, the boot needs to make contact with the ball just a moment after the ball has rebounded from the ground.

The same approach applies for goal-line drop-outs and drop-outs on the 20-metre line after an attempt at goal has failed but

has been kicked dead. Clearly, a drop goal specialist is a real asset, as the further he can kick the ball, the better it is for the defending side.

Kicking for territory

While goalkicking is now so crucial — it has helped Manly, the Bulldogs and Norths immeasurably in recent years — kicking in general play is equally vital tactically. Ricky Stuart is a master at this, with an incredible array of kicks; his ability to get the ball to break towards the sideline is quite uncanny.

Today accuracy is demanded and expected from any team's designated kickers. If kicking for territory and position from a defensive position, the kick must not roll dead. It needs to be weighted to stay in the field of play, angled away from defensive players so the chasers have as much time as possible to corner the player running the kick back. To kick the ball straight at a fullback or winger is a waste, giving the chase no time to close down the angles or prevent easy metres being gained.

When kicking for the line from a penalty it must be stressed

The old and the new of Australian goalkicking. Kangaroo legend Mal Meninga (above left) was no better than a hit-and-hope proposition as a goalkicker in the later years of his playing career. But Illawarra and Australian winger Rod Wishart provided a dramatic improvement in the Kangaroos' success rate with his more acceptable round the corner style. Wishart regularly ranks among the Winfield Cup's most accurate kickers.

again — as it has been in the Penalties chapter — that the kick must find touch, even if it means sacrificing some distance.

Attacking kicks

The range of attacking kicks is another facet of the game that players need to perfect. Generally it is the halves who have these skills. On attack, the common aim is to weight a kick to sit in the in-goal area, forcing a defender to kick or push the ball dead; or, if he fields it, the goal is to tackle him before he can advance the ball back into the field of play. In any of those eventualities, there will be a goal-line drop-out, so ensuring another set of six tackles for the attacking side.

The *bomb* remains a potent attacking weapon, although it too needs to be placed accurately. If it should land in-goal and there is no one putting pressure on competing for the ball, it only needs to be caught on the full by a defender and it is a tap re-start on the 20-metre line for the defending team. Bombs placed to land near the goal-line are more prevalent and seem to produce better results on attack.

The *chip kick* over the defensive line is an option which finds favour with a lot of sides. Very few players are as devastating with it as Phil Blake. He has used it many times in his career, running at full pace after being put through a hole, he can chip a kick over the top of the defence to land in the in-goal area and then surge through for the touchdown. The *grubber kick* along the ground is often used with the same effect.

Ricky Stuart and Brett Mullins have worked a combination with their bomb and chip kick plays. Stuart chips or bombs the defence and Mullins has made a habit of charging through to collect them on the full for spectacular tries.

The crossfield bombs can work perfectly, too, as Allan Langer has done with Willie Carne many times and the grubber through a defensive line usually stretches a side.

What all these kicks require is a high skill factor which can only be honed by constant practice. And you will find plenty of capable practitioners around today who have all-round ability as team kickers. Stuart might be king but Langer's short kicking game is superb. Greg Alexander, Gene Ngamu and Phil Blake have special kicking qualities, as do Jason Taylor, Cliff Lyons, Matthew Ridge, Terry Lamb, John Simon, Laurie Daley and the Johns brothers at Newcastle, along with Shaun Edwards, Frano Botica, Garry Schofield, Deryck Fox, Bobby Goulding and others in England.

It is all very well to be able to run with the football and pass it. But today, teams also need more than one player who can kick it as well, both for goal and for position.

Following pages: Since starting his league career with Wigan in 1990, Frano Botica has developed into one of the greatest goalkickers and points-scorers the game has seen.

Below: Warrior Gene Ngamu has worked on developing the all-round game now required of a top-line stand-off. Kicking is one of the demands of the position; principally this involves clearing the ball on the final tackle, as Ngamu does here.

10

VIDEO EZY
STEEDEN
INTERNATIONAL

RUNNING

The variety of your attack must confuse the defence and it will fail to do this if you are stereotyped and run into the attack at the same point in the backline each time you come in.

Graham Eadie (Australian International, 1973–79)

Playing the ball, tackling, passing and kicking are all integral aspects of the game but a very basic and obvious requirement is the ability to run. And, because running is the one quality everyone needs to play the game, it is easy to take it for granted and to fail to pay it due attention.

In off-season training today, coaching staff will put a lot of effort into weight-training and related strength areas, but there is also loads of effort put into aspects of running. Not just in the sense of running to build up aerobic fitness and to improve stamina levels; it is far more specialised than that.

With most top clubs, the trainers concentrate on speed work. You work on your speed from a standing start and over shorter and longer distances; you can also train to improve your speed in moving up and back, as you will need to in the defensive line all season.

Opposite: The demands on front row forwards are far different from those on outside backs. For Canberra's John Lomax there is a constant need to confront the defence, so the ball will often be locked under one arm with the leading arm used to fend off or hold off tacklers.

Right: Running with the football is a science, but Phil Blake turns it into an art. Confronted by Brisbane's Michael Hancock, the Warriors fullback can put on a lethal swerve or a step, and he has the fend ready if necessary.

Effort is also put into your ability to change direction at speed with the ball in hand, and without it when you are forced to change course after being wrong-footed in defence. There are plenty of drills designed to improve speed and technique. But the speed work is only one part of it; in league it is all about how to run and where to run.

The 'how' is fundamental yet highly important. When running with the ball, avoid running in an upright or erect fashion. Defenders will find it very easy to back-slam a ball carrier who offers them that sort of target. What is needed is a style where the ball carrier leans slightly forward. That way, if he is running at pace, he can drive forward with his legs and have a fair chance

Four of Australia's best running the ball at the defence, but all with different requirements and different skills.
Above left: Brad Fittler is one of the game's most explosive running talents. He has excellent acceleration and an electric sidestep.

Above: Until he retired, Mal Meninga had created a deserved reputation as perhaps the most feared runner in the world.

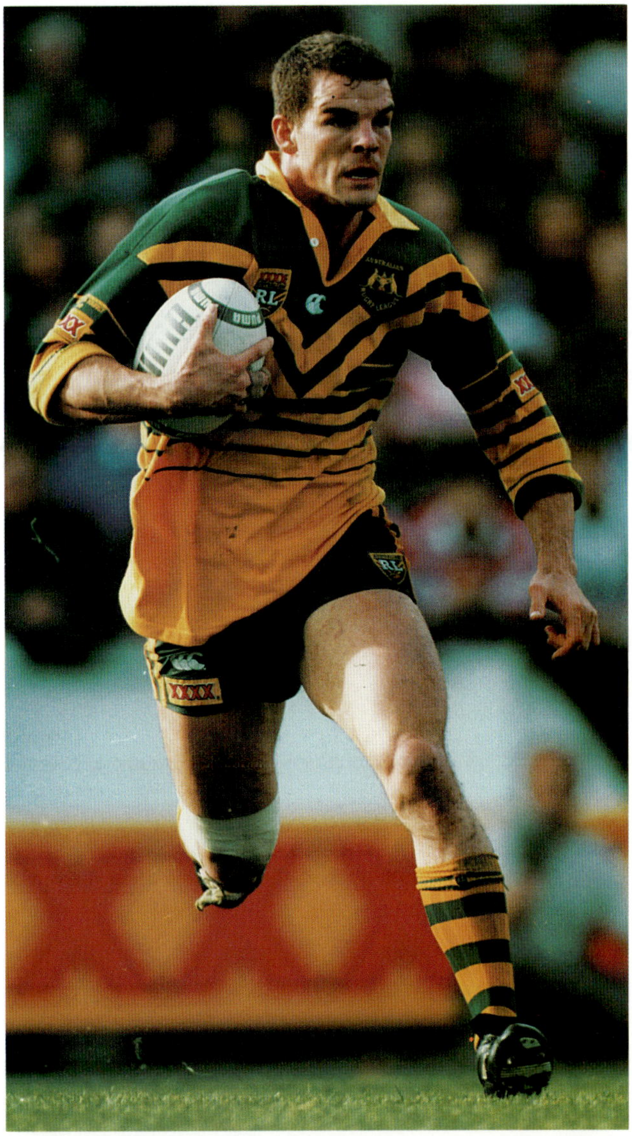

Above: For a no-frills runner of the football, Ian Roberts is in the top echelon. While gangling and awkward in his movement at times, that also makes him the danger he is running at a defence.

Above right: One of the world's great runners from dummy half — hooker Steve Walters. He scurries out of dummy half brilliantly to stretch any defence around the ruck, especially when he's close to the line.

of making forward progress, or falling forward, despite the attention of tacklers.

Generally speaking, players should also run with the ball in two hands. Playmakers in the style of Ricky Stuart, Greg Alexander, Shaun Edwards and others will nearly always do that because they are trying to create doubt in the defence. By showing the ball, they can dummy and feint, perhaps create a gap and then suddenly have the chance to run through it, or put another runner through it.

Forwards hitting the ball up to the defence don't have that option so often. When confronted with tacklers, it is often the best course to put the ball under one arm and use the other to try and fend them off, or to hit and spin, while also trying to protect themselves from swinging arms, elbows, forearms and the like.

Another vital part of the 'how to run' equation is pace. Always have the intention to run at pace with the ball. Don't cruise or coast onto a pass and up to the defensive line; there is no healthy future in it. Not everyone in league will take a pass at pace, for obvious reasons. Inside players might take the ball flat-footed because their sole intention is to move the ball wide as quickly as possible; for them to run onto the pass simply cuts down the space available as they would come closer to meeting the converging defensive line.

But anyone taking on the defence, should do so at pace. That is how it is with speed merchants like Steve Renouf, Willie Carne, Phil Blake, Sean Hoppe, Brett Mullins, Martin Offiah and so many others. One of the key elements in their try-scoring success is that they hit a pass at pace. They have natural speed in any

Below left: One of the arts of the game, more so for play-makers, is to run with the ball held in two hands. It creates uncertainty, and in his Wigan days, Andy Gregory bamboozled plenty of defences that way.

Below: Front row forwards will generally hit the ball up without looking to pass, but that is changing. Here, Great Britain's Karl Harrison runs to the defensive line, twists his torso and pops a nice pass for his support.

case but they accentuate the value of that by taking the ball at speed. It sounds simple enough but it isn't always observed, even by many first grade players.

Pace is never more important than when running onto a short pass or slipped ball in traffic. It is one of rugby league's most exciting qualities to see fleet-footed players taking what we call a short ball off a playmaker; it is known as running off a player. Say Greg Alexander takes or runs the ball right up to the defensive line and then, as he is about to be hit in a tackle, he flips out a short pass to a player supporting or running off him. That player might be a quick second-rower like Tony Tatupu, maybe a Phil Blake or even a Dean Bell. The timing of the run is critical but, even with several defenders around, it works with devastating effect.

The player receiving will run on a line within a metre or so of the ball carrier, depending where the evident hole is in the defence. Sometimes the two players involved might even brush

Below: Always hungry to run, hungry to back up and hungry to score tries — Wigan halfback/stand-off Shaun Edwards. Like all the best attackers, he must have pace, but most of all he knows when and where to run, with or without the football.

Below right: One of the most breath-taking running sights in the game is Martin Offiah on one of his all-too-familiar 'length of the field' dashes for a try.

each other, that is how close the transfer point is. Done at speed and with the timing spot on, defenders have a hell of a job stopping a player running off another one in this way. Of course, it also requires a large dose of confidence from the support player to run at a hole which might not seem to be there at times. The number one rule is to watch the ball. Take a look at the defenders and you're gone.

Pace alone won't always reap dividends. In the first place, the player looking to use his pace to beat the defence, or to score a try, needs to receive a fair pass (see the next chapter), but he also needs a reasonable mastery of the game's evasive skills when running with the football.

Running straight at a defender even at exceptional pace is often pointless, unless the would-be defender simply can't tackle. Then again, it never seemed to worry Mal Meninga or Olsen Filipaina; they were exceptional with their ability to burst through and bump off tacklers through sheer bulk, strength and pace. It wasn't an accident that they were always regarded as two of the most difficult players to tackle.

Presuming opponents can tackle — and most rugby league players at top level can — the ball carrier needs the ability to beat a man. Sometimes that can be achieved by straight running if you hit the pass at a certain angle, say taking a line on a slight angle back towards the direction the ball is coming from. It can be enough to beat a defender on the inside and take you clear.

Kiwi winger Sean Hoppe is a wonderfully balanced runner. With a characteristic lean forward, he mixes sharp pace and strength to pose a constant danger when running with the ball.

More often, though, a change of pace, a dummy, a side-step, a swerve or a fend will be needed. Maybe a combination of the lot at times. The hit and spin, or hit and roll, technique is another running tactic which can beat defences.

The key with the side-step is to do it at pace, to be able to explode away having stepped a defender. Without that acceleration, the value of beating a man with a step will be lost. You give the beaten defender time to reorganise himself and track you down, and you also give the cover valuable fractions of a second to close you down.

The swerve is highly effective, a potent weapon used by many fullbacks, wingers and centres. Martin Offiah has a brilliant swerve. So do Steve Renouf and Brett Mullins, and many more could be included. The in-and-away swerve is the most dangerous. If you can convince a tackler you are heading infield, forcing him to hesitate or check, then you are on the way. You feint to veer infield, then drive off your inside leg and arc towards the outside at full speed. It is an exciting way to burn off a defender, even more so if it finishes with a try.

The change of pace has similar results. The idea is to lull the defender into thinking you are running at a lower gear; then, as

CITIBANK

he moves in for the tackle, accelerate to top pace to deceive him. Hopefully, he has been left behind, or at worst barely managed to touch you.

Dummy half running is a specialist area. The initial requirement is to watch and pick the ball up after it has been played. A low to the ground, scampering style of running is needed to clear away from the markers and hopefully to exploit any gap there might be immediately beyond the markers.

When wingers run with the ball on their touchline, they always need to be aware of where the line is. If there is ever doubt or fear of being taken into touch by the cover defence, it is wise to veer infield immediately, dropping the inside shoulder, driving off the outside leg and bracing to withstand the force of tacklers trying to take you across the touchline.

Forwards have greater physical demands running with the ball because, while in possession, they can expect to be hit by two, three or even four tacklers. Ball security is their priority

Below left: For more than a decade, John Kirwan ran on instinct for the All Blacks. Then, as a 30-year-old retired rugby union winger, he became a dramatic signing for the Warriors. In his Warriors debut — in the reserve grade against North Sydney — he soon had his fend out.

Below: From St Helens and on to Wigan, Gary Connolly has developed into an integral component in Great Britain's game.

Right: From Wigan to the Warriors, Dean Bell brought his professional skills back home in 1995. What he gave the Warriors as a runner was an extra forward, a man who would dig it in and hit the ball out from deep defence, and a man who would run the ball at the defensive line on early tackles. But he also gave them a man who could do his share on attack as a centre, unloading some lovely passes, especially to his right winger Sean Hoppe.

but, in hitting the ball up at the defensive line, a forward-leaning style of running is paramount. It is an advantage to the team if a player doing a regular hit-up is able to fall forwards in the tackle because he then has a much better chance of being able to play the ball quickly. At the same time, even forwards carting the ball up need to be able to make the ball available. They should look to free their arms as the tacklers come in, so they can off load a pass if it is on.

That covers some of the territory involving running with the ball. Running into position to receive the ball requires careful attention as well. It is a co-ordinated activity involving the hands, feet, eyes, brain and body, and it helps to be given a reasonable pass. That won't always be the case, but as long as a player concentrates carefully, he can collect most passes, even the ones that are a little too low or high. Watch the ball and just about anything is possible. You should expect to catch the ball between the chest and the stomach but be prepared for it to come to you anywhere.

Left: Jonathan Davies wasn't often able to express his value as a running footballer when he was with the struggling Welsh rugby union side. That all changed when he moved to Widnes and then Warrington. He has lightning acceleration and great speed over a distance, as the Australians found out in the first Ashes test at Wembley in 1994, when he outpaced Brett Mullins to score the matchwinner.

Opposite: Much of New Zealand's best rugby league talent is in England.

Top left: Leeds centre Kevin Iro mixes all the running skills to dazzling effect.

Top right: Craig Innes specialises in running more directly at the defence than his Leeds centre partner Kevin Iro. He benefits as an attacker through good basic speed and strength to match.

Bottom left: Wigan tuned Frano Botica up for league by starting him on the wing. His goalkicking class aside, he has developed into a gifted runner at either stand-off or halfback.

Bottom right: Look at Tawera Nikau with the ball and it's easy to see why he causes concern for defenders. The ball is in two hands again, and like the great loose forwards, he's a playmaker first and a runner second these days.

Where to run is all about angles of attack and what move is on. A fullback should look to enter the line in all sorts of places. Maybe he comes in outside the inside or outside centre; perhaps inside one of those players to take an inside ball. Other times he might be a decoy runner or he might loom up outside one of the wingers. There needs to be variety just as there does when wingers run into the action. A regulation move is to bring the blindside winger in from the scrum, running across field to set the play the ball up more towards the centre of the field. On the

Left: Given some room by the Western Suburbs defence, Warriors prop Hitro Okesene is able to swerve and also hand off a tackle.

Bottom left: The timing of the fend is crucial. Western Suburbs centre Ken McGuinness has it just right, much to Hitro Okesene's embarrassment, in the Magpies' Ericsson Stadium clash against the Warriors in 1995.

Opposite: The man the Warriors let go. Henry Paul wanted to play for Wigan and the Warriors did a trade to let him out of his contract with them. In the process, they lost one of the most dazzling runners around. For one so young, Paul has astonishing poise and balance on attack — he glides, he can jink about, he steps and swerves. He lacks nothing when running with the ball.

Following pages: The perfect example of how to run with the football in traffic. Warriors second rower Tony Tatupu locks the ball under his right arm, leaving his left free to push down the tackling arm of a defender.

same play another time he can look to straighten up. The options are endless but where to run on attack needs to be carefully judged — and it needs to be varied.

While running with the ball is the attraction of the game, running without it is by far the main activity for all players. Running up and then back in defence; running back into position after the ball has been lost on attack or through a handover; running up in a line chasing a kick; running to back up after moving the ball to a support. The game barely stops running for 80 minutes. The committed and dedicated player won't stop running either.

PRO-tection
3

LION RED
11
Mobil
9

NSETT
MMI

PASSING

Never move towards the player to whom you are passing. Give him the benefit of the space between the two of you.

Rod Reddy (Australian International, 1978–82)

Opposite: This is the way to do it. With his arms stretched way out in front, Warriors second rower Tony Tatupu is unworried by a thigh-high tackle, and is able to pass the ball to any team-mate in support.

Rugby league players need all manner of qualities and skills, but the ability to pass the football is one of the game's true art forms; and one requiring some degree of proficiency, if not mastery, in all positions.

The first inclination and desire when starting to play league as a youngster is to run with the ball. It takes time to appreciate that there is more to the game, and to realise it is movement of the ball through the hands which has so much to do with making league the spectacle it is.

At the highest level, the passing demands vary from position to position. Front rowers have generally been entrusted with taking the ball up on early tackles and so are rarely required to pass; their first duty is to make some forward progress and look to follow it with a quick play the ball.

That was certainly the pattern under the 5-metre rule. Today, the demands have changed a little, evolving to a point where

Right: Warriors captain Dean Bell keeps his arms and the ball free. It can't always be achieved, but whenever a player is about to be tackled every effort should be made to keep the arms free so that a pass can be given.

Left: Two studies of Greg Alexander's passing style. The Warriors' halfback has run up to the defensive line (top), committing Brisbane's Michael Hancock, and is aiming to put a runner into space with his pass. He pivots (bottom), taking a small step back towards the direction he's received the ball from, as he unloads a flighted pass to his backline. There are few halfbacks with better ability at throwing the selective pass.

Opposite: A classic study of how to pass the football. Australian and Canberra stand-off Laurie Daley is one of the game's best passers. He has the ball firmly held, he's balanced, he's watching his target, his arms are extended; everything is in order for an ideal pass. Daley's also proficient at passing to both sides.

props need to be far more mobile to take advantage of the 10-metre rule. They are also being encouraged to free the ball up instead of being programmed to take the tackle. Kiwi John Lomax was a real example with Canberra in 1994 when he started slipping lots of passes. For that, credit the 10-metre rule and the extra room it creates; props can now confidently take the ball to the defensive line and give a short pass to a support.

The truth was, the old-styled ball-playing prop — like an Artie Beetson — had become almost extinct, with front-rowers being told their only purpose was to take the ball up and forget about

XXXX
PUMA

LION
RED
KIWIS
PUMA
RUGBY LEAGUE
"PRO"
PUMA

Right: A study of totally focussed concentration. Wigan halfback Shaun Edwards is not letting any outside influence divert his attention; all that matters is the ball as he waits to catch it. This is what you call watching the ball.

Opposite: Halfbacks are so heavily involved in the game today that they must have the best passing game in their team. Kiwi scrumhalf Gary Freeman fills the bill for every team he plays in. While he doesn't boast a pass as long as Ricky Stuart's specials, he is still a quality passer. Here, he is doing everything right; he is poised to make a good pass on the move to his supports.

the rest. Brent Todd used to do that sort of job for Canberra and the Kiwis; so did Dane Sorensen for Cronulla and New Zealand. It was the smart way to play the game under the 5-metre rule yet, before he went to Australia, Dane Sorensen had been a clever ball player in Auckland. That props are now encouraged to remove the shackles is a plus. There are times when they need to give a team forward progress with solid hit-ups but still be able to loosen up and move the ball when it is on.

There is a lot of skill involved in passing or slipping the ball when there is so much traffic around. Front-row forwards can have two or three tacklers trying to bring them down but often they will be able to keep one arm free, holding the ball, to pop it back to a player backing up. That sort of play can really stretch a defensive line; if two or three defenders are drawn to a prop and he unloads in the tackle, there should be some holes somewhere.

The back-row forwards have a mix of passing demands. In the same manner as props, they look to pop short passes, or off-load in the tackle, but many of them also have a brief to drift wide of the ruck, where they might operate almost like another centre. In that regard, a player of the calibre of Bradley Clyde has a touch of everything. His passing game, in the course of a match, can encompass all needs. He will do as many hit-ups as the big men, unload in the tackle or perhaps hit and spin and move the ball on. But he will also be found lurking out wide where he is capable of throwing a pass as good as any centre can for his wingers. No surprise then that Canberra have actually played him as a centre.

The forward with the greatest responsibility for passing is the hooker. Together with the halves, he forms the vital combination for ensuring an attack flows. Essentially it is the hooker who is assigned to fill the dummy half role, so clearing the ball effectively is mandatory for the man in the No 9 jersey. The onus on him is to move the ball smoothly to the first receiver — often the halfback — if he is not having a dart himself. There are plenty of hookers with a very good pass — the Walters brothers, Steve and Kerrod, Benny Elias and Auckland Warriors Duane Mann and Syd Eru, and Wigan's Martin Dermott, who has one of the quickest passes off the ground.

What a side needs is a quick dummy half pass to give the halfback as much time as possible to pick up his runners. If the halfback is not at first receiver and the call is for a regulation

Below: One of the hooker's main roles is the pass from dummy half. Brisbane's Kerrod Walters provides the text-book version with his right foot planted and pointing in the direction he is passing; his weight, evenly distributed giving him balance and his hands pointed down the ball. He shouldn't have a problem giving a good pass.

hit-up, the dummy half's pass needs to be flat — as close to a forward pass as legally possible — and in front of the player taking it. At the same time, delivery from dummy half depends on players timing their runs properly.

The halfback and stand-off (five-eighth) throw the most vital passes in most games. After all, they are responsible for firing an attack and, if they are not in tune, the team often suffers. It is these two players, especially in sides like Canberra (Ricky Stuart and Laurie Daley), Brisbane (Allan Langer and Kevin Walters) and the Warriors (Greg Alexander and Gene Ngamu), who need to have a full repertoire of passes.

A real strength is the long spiral pass to cut out players and pick up a target perhaps up to 30 metres away. No one executes that pass better than Ricky Stuart, evidenced by the number of tries his long ball specials have laid on. But the halves also need to know how to weight their passes, both the long and short ones. They also have to be adept at popping up a reverse pass

Below left and right: The proliferation of rugby union players in rugby league has also introduced a different approach to passing. Wearing the Welsh league team's test strip, Jonathan Davies (left) has the ball available, ready to pick up a runner coming around behind him. Frano Botica (right), Wigan's former All Black and double international, started his league career on the wing but his passing skills were always one of his strengths and soon saw him playing at both halfback and stand-off.

Left: Kiwi halfback Aaron Whittaker doesn't seem to be going by the book here. Playing for Wakefield Trinity in England, he is clearly eyeing up where he wants to pass but he seems to be doing so before he has secured the ball in the first place. Always watch the ball when catching a pass, then, once you have it, look for your target.

Opposite: The right way to take a pass. Playing for the then Canterbury-Bankstown Bulldogs in 1994 (to become the Sydney Bulldogs in 1995), Kiwi Jason Williams has been thrown a slightly high pass, but there is no risk of him dropping it because his eyes are focussed on the ball, not preoccupied with where he's looking to run, or checking out where any defenders are stationed.

when it is called for, or they can dummy to the open and then flick the ball back to a runner on the inside. They can often throw what is called a face ball, a pass which seems intended for the player immediately outside but instead passes right in front of him and goes to the next player out. The halves, and especially the halfbacks, orchestrate the game with their passing and it can be a joy to watch.

Wally Lewis was a legendary passer of the football. Some New Zealanders would rate the great Roger Bailey as maybe even better in the 1960s and early 1970s, for he could flick out long passes which always seemed to travel flat and straight to their target — he was a freak passer.

Obviously the goal is to hold the ball in two hands and be able to pass it safely and accurately using both hands. That is

XURY
ACHES

Two examples of the front rower's classic one-handed off-load.
Above: In his Widnes years, long-time Kiwi prop Kurt Sorensen was one of the most skilled and feared front rowers in England. Using his left arm to hold off a tackler, he has his right free to flip a pass to his support.

not always possible, not when one hand is being used to ward off tacklers, or hold them at bay. In this case, the arm furthest away from the defender(s) cradles the ball and it can be made available by being flipped out to a supporting player.

That is usually the case for forwards, and centres often find themselves in the same situation. Generally, a centre strives to set up his winger by creating as much space as possible before unloading the ball. You can't always get the ball to your winger with a regular pass; defenders do have a habit of blocking the way so you have to improvise. Maybe you try a lob pass over the top, perhaps a basketball type pass or there is the one around behind a defender.

A pass around a defender can give you the greatest satisfaction. I was able to get one such pass to Sean Hoppe in the Warriors' Winfield Cup debut against Brisbane. I tried to take on Michael Hancock and Wendell Sailor and, when there was no way through, I was able to reach my

Above right: Cronulla prop Danny Lee has done the same. Pushing off a Manly defender, he has the ball well out of reach in his left hand ready to unload. One-handed passes have a higher risk element but it is often the only way forwards can push a pass.

hands through behind Sailor and pass the ball around his back to Sean. It worked perfectly. Many forwards also use that sort of pass, sometimes flicking it around the back one-handed.

Wingers shouldn't ignore the value of the pass either. It is not a case of giving them the ball and then seeing how far they can go. The good wingers are conscious of maintaining continuity on attack and, while they look to make progress, they are also alert to keeping the ball alive. With fullbacks it is much the same. The complete ones don't merely come into the backline and ultimately take the tackle, they are skilful enough to give an attack real thrust and then link up with supports.

The timing of the pass is even more important than the type of pass, or who to pass to. All factors need to be in harmony. A runner who arrives too early will force the passer to throw a forward pass, or to throw a pass which the runner has to reach back for. Arrive too late and the pass will usually end up on the

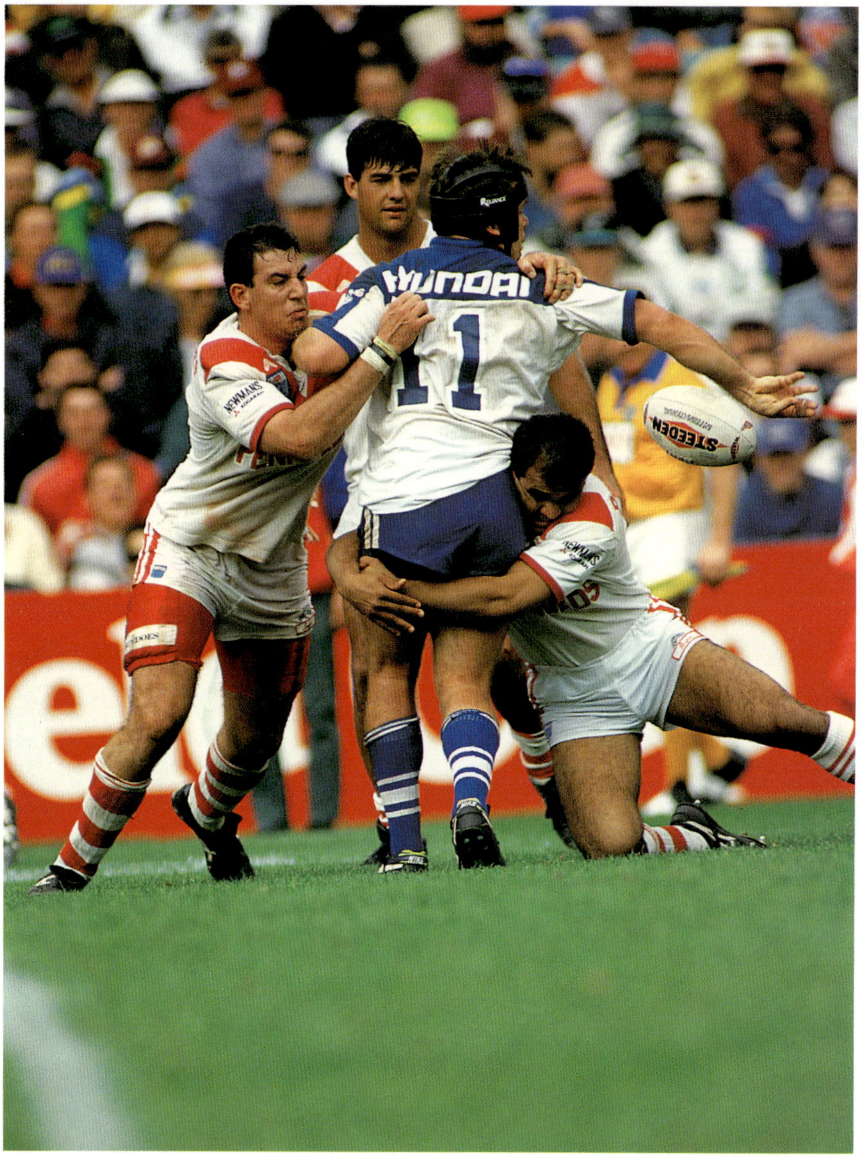

Left: Canterbury-Bankstown's Darren Smith defies St George's double-teaming in the tackle to pop a pass out the back door. It has to be a one-handed effort but the pass does work if due care is taken. It's a passing skill that needs to be worked on.

Opposite: A pass in the tackle doesn't always need to be a one-hander. Look at this from St George's Jeff Hardy. He has gone for the over-the-top two-hander to out-smart North Sydney's defence.

ground, or the runner will reach in vain and knock on.

The ideal pass is flat and thrown at reasonable speed; not too hard, but a solid pass. Apart from the type and speed of the pass, there is one rule which always must be observed: don't pass if it is not on. The ball carrier is better to hold the ball and use a tackle if there is a risk of losing possession. Only on the last tackle, when you have been blocked out of the kick option, should you entertain throwing risky passes. The same applies in the dying moments if your team is behind and looking for a matchwinner, but, in general, reckless passing is one of the worst sins in the game, and not easily excused by any self-respecting coach.

tyRail

CITY FORD

Opposite:
Top left: The one-handed flick back is often an option for forwards, as it is here for Canberra's Quentin Pongia.

Top right: Big Eastern Suburbs forward Craig Salvatori takes the crunch of an attempted ball-and-all tackle from Balmain's Steve Edmed — but he still gets his pass away.

Bottom left: For deft passing skills and a bit of sleight of hand, Shane Cooper has been difficult to top in his years with St Helens.

Bottom right: The nature of rugby league demands it — the ability to unload the ball in the tackle. Leeds stand-off Graham Holroyd is fighting off the combined presence of Bradford Northern's Deryck Fox and David Heron but has still managed to pop out a pass, and that breaks any team.

Right: The ideal illustration of the draw and pass technique. Manly's fullback Matthew Ridge knows where his support is, so he has fixed on Penrith's Brad Fittler, looking to 'straighten him' in defence and create a hole for anyone running off him.

Following pages: George Mann has always had a reputation as a ball-playing forward. He has proved that with both Leeds and St Helens. About to hit the ground in Andy Platt's tackle, he is still poised to flick a pass.

Passing, and the link or combination between players, is undoubtedly sharpened by constant match play. The experience of players working together will develop the passing game but, like any aspect of rugby league, it is also helped by regular practice. One of the most fulfilling experiences in rugby league is laying on a pass that produces a try. It could be a pass early in a movement which opens up possibilities, or it might be the final transfer before the try is scored. But it takes hours of practice to perfect the art and savour that delight on a regular basis.

ERN ROCK

OPTUS
BORAL CONCRETE
SAAB

DEFENCE

In attack, I'm flexible...but I'm very demanding on defence. With the defensive side of the game, the players must do exactly what I want them to do. I'm not flexible with my defensive plan.

John Monie (Auckland Warriors Coach)

The defensive side of rugby league needs to be broken down into two basic areas — the art of tackling itself and organising your defence in a tactical sense. It is all very well to be able to tackle, but all the tackling skill in the world will count for little if you are not part of a cohesive and united defensive screen or pattern. Of course, a team's defence will work efficiently only if the level of tackling ability is there in the first place; but if players leave a hole in the defensive line, no tackle will save their side.

Under Graham Lowe, and then John Monie, Wigan managed to revolutionise the defensive side of the game in England. Until the mid 1980s, English club sides had a lax attitude to the game's defensive requirements and because Lowe started, and then Monie further refined, improved discipline and tactical awareness in this area, Wigan were able to enjoy a significant advantage.

However, the change in attitude did not please everyone. When John Monie first started at Wigan, some fans complained that he concentrated too much on defence — even though the team was still winning! It took a long time for the other teams to compete with Wigan's defensive standards, and former Kiwi and Wigan player Graeme West continued the tradition as the Riversiders' new coach in the 1994–95 season.

After John Monie accepted the job to coach the Warriors in 1995, and I agreed to join him as captain, I knew what to expect from him defensively. He has standards he won't compromise when he's considering the defensive aspects of the game.

So, it didn't sit too well with him when the Warriors' defence revealed some significant shortcomings in the first two matches of the 1995 Winfield Cup season.

Left: Brisbane winger Wendell Sailor first, the rest nowhere. Balmain's defence is effectively non-existent, the cover seemingly not within spitting distance of the Broncos' man. No side can afford to be this drastically out-manoeuvred at Winfield Cup level; it usually carries a heavy cost — a try.

Above: The straight line of defence — Illawarra's players in defensive formation poised to rush up to meet the opposition. While the line might be formed straight enough, it also needs to move up in the same shape; the moment one or two players fail to maintain the desired even line across the field, holes will be there for the team in possession.

Our first match against Brisbane was a night never to be forgotten, creating history for New Zealand rugby league. But there was no escaping the fact, when the game was analysed later, that we should have won the match instead of losing it 25–22; and one of the reasons we failed to win was our defence. It lost shape and the defensive line developed some chinks; we weren't moving up, we weren't marking up properly and we began to give Allan Langer far too much room to operate in. After sitting on him for close to an hour, we lost intensity and allowed him to run the game — and eventually win it for Brisbane.

A week later, against Illawarra, the defence was even worse. Quite simply, we made it easy for Illawarra and, as everyone kept saying, we learned some fairly painful lessons that day about life in the Winfield Cup. Our attack actually kept us in contention in that match but, if we were to win games, we knew then — if we hadn't before — that our defence had to match our attack.

There are flaws common to weak defence, over and above poor tackling. Too often teams sit back in defence and wait, instead of moving up — one of the most elementary rules in defence. When you wait, you hand all the advantage to the side in possession; they can make a cheap 10 metres on every tackle when not challenged and that generates a roll-on effect that can become an irresistible force.

The other equally important requirement in the modern game is to have your marker defence precisely organised. Defending teams are entitled to have two markers at the play the ball. One stands — or marks up — directly in front of the tackled player as he plays the ball. The second marker stands directly behind the player marking up. As long as there are always two markers who are correctly aligned — they can't be standing to the side of the tackled player — the team on the defence is on the way to mastering this vital aspect of the game.

The markers work to cover options on each side of the play the ball; one ready to protect any raids on the left, the other set to cover the right. Sound marker defence is aimed at minimising the attacking side's chances of grabbing territory through runs from dummy half, especially when you are playing against the likes of the Walters brothers, Kerrod and Steve, who are masters at taking advantage of any lapses.

Below: Canterbury's Mark Nixon (left) and Brendon Tuuta provide the regulation defensive screen to cut off Auckland's Tea Ropati in New Zealand's 1993 first division final. Tuuta shapes to knock down Ropati's intended fend and take the Aucklander high, while Nixon moves in from the other side to take Ropati low — the classic up-and-down tackling approach.

Teams often fail to have two markers in position. One factor can be that players have not perfected the technique of holding the tackled player down long enough so that the defence can reorganise. It is a skill to know how far to go with this and still not incur a penalty, but tacklers do their side no favours if they allow the ball carrier to play the ball too quickly.

Much of this comes back to tackling techniques. The aim for the defending side is to put the ball carrier on the ground, so slowing his ability to play the ball swiftly; and it is better still if the defender (or defenders) can finish on top of the player in possession, rather than being trapped underneath. That way, the attacking side is being held up sufficiently for the defending side to reorganise; to be caught underneath a tackled player renders that defender useless for the next play because, most times, he won't be able to rejoin the defensive line, or fill one of the marker spots, before the ball is played.

Above: A case study of using logic in defence. The basic equation shows three Brisbane defenders in the frame, faced with five St George players. But rather than all being drawn to the ball carrier, Kerrod Walters (left) and Terry Matterson (right) have hung off ready to cover any possibility of the ball being unloaded in the tackle. While it is important to stop the ball carrier, to over-commit players to the man running the ball — especially in this instance — would simply leave too many gaps in an already stretched defensive line.

Defence is also about ensuring you have numbered off correctly, on each side of the ruck; if the attacking side has five men lined out on the blind side, you need to match the numbers. Someone should always be counting, always looking where the defensive line is thin or is being out-manoeuvred by the opposition trying to pull in an extra man. Managing the defence comes down to communication; if you spot a danger area, call out. It won't fix itself unless you alert someone to the problem.

There are different ways to approach defence. The most obvious is straight man-to-man marking. There is also the sliding defence technique, where the defending side ensures the defensive line moves, or slides, across the field in the direction the attacking side is moving the ball, forcing them towards the sideline.

Compressed defence is where the defending side crunches in or compacts the defensive line by pushing players in from the touchline; the intention is to create a more intense defensive screen around the ruck area to guard against raids up the middle of the field. Simultaneously, the defensive line operates in an umbrella fashion by moving up swiftly on the outsides and trying to force the side in possession to turn the ball inside, where the concentrated defence should be. There is an accompanying risk to this tactic, though; the attacking side can cause embarrassment if the ball can be moved swiftly enough along the line to outflank the outer edges of the compressed defensive line.

Right: If a side's defensive line is breached or outflanked — and Canterbury-Bankstown winger Brett Dallas has done that to Newcastle here — the cover defence needs to come into effect. Often that will appear in the shape of a halfback operating a second line of defence, moving across behind the frontline defence in a sweeper's role as the attacking side moves the ball. But back-row forwards can also be expected to provide cover on defence, as can wingers who can come off their own wing to stop an attack on the opposite side.

TDK
PENFOLDS

POWER'S
POWER'S
the

Right: Western Suburbs fullback Andrew Leeds extends the Warriors' defence, dragging loose forward Tony Tuimavave across in cover. For his part, Tuimavave is trying to negate Leeds' chance of beating him on the outside but Leeds also has the option of giving an inside ball to centre Ken McGuinness, who's shaping to cut back to support his fullback on his inside.

Opposite top: St George have their defensive network in place to handle Canberra's Noa Nadruku. Fullback Mick Potter has him lined up, centre Mark Coyne (No 3) moves in on him too, and Brad Mackay (right) is covering the scene.

Opposite bottom: On early tackles, it is vital to defend in numbers. By throwing at least two men into the tackle, the player and the ball should be locked up. The value of a third man in the tackle is to ensure the ball carrier is put on the ground to eliminate the chance of a quick play the ball. At the same time, putting three defenders on the ball carrier will leave the defensive line short, unless one of the three can move back very quickly.

Following pages: The Leeds defence copes with the threat posed by Wigan's Frano Botica in the 1994 Challenge Cup final at Wembley. The impression is that Wigan captain Dean Bell is unmarked on Botica's left but Craig Innes, about to smother Botica from behind, and Ellery Hanley have the situation well under control.

Wherever the ball is played, the defensive line must be set 10 metres back (except when the play the ball is within 10 metres of the defending team's goal-line). It can't be stressed enough that this line needs to be straight and that it also needs to move up to meet the attacking side as a straight line; moving back after each tackle, the same should apply.

It is common with modern-day defences to have the defending fullback standing in the defensive line when a scrum is put down. The idea is that it negates the possibility of bringing the attacking fullback into the backline to create an overlap. But it does leave the defending team vulnerable to a kick over the top, so the wingers have to be on the look-out to cover the possibility of a kick.

The fullback and wingers have another common defensive responsibility — to drop back for kicks from the team in possession. For wingers, that means dropping out of the defensive line and covering the touchlines after the fifth tackle, thereby being stationed to field any kick for position. Wingers also need to be poised to support the fullback when he is defending high kicks or bombs. Often the wingers have to 'defuse' the bombs themselves, so fullbacks and wingers find a significant aspect of their defensive ability involves the talent to leap off the ground to catch the ball. They also need to be quick to turn and scamper to cover grubber kicks or chip kicks into the in-goal area, the ones Allan Langer, Greg Alexander and Ricky Stuart like to employ.

TETLEY
FOSTE

NORWEB

Left: The best players are always a threat on attack, even close to the ruck where the defence might be expected to be more difficult to pierce. Great Britain forwards Andy Platt (left) and Billy McGinty (right) weren't quick enough to close down the gap Kiwi captain Gary Freeman spotted in the second test in 1992.

Opposite top: All sides need a back-up when the frontline defence fails, that's why halfbacks often operate in a sweeping role. Here, it is all set to work for Australia in the first test against New Zealand in 1991. Replacement halfback Clayton Friend has stepped Australian loose forward Bradley Clyde, but Allan Langer provides the insurance, coming across as the second line of defence.

Opposite bottom: The referee has signalled the final tackle, and Western Suburbs hooker Jim Serdaris has cornered Warriors stand-off Gene Ngamu. Pushing him to the outside, Serdaris is looking to prevent Ngamu putting in a kick on the last tackle or beating him by running the ball.

Wingers have an added responsibility when positioning themselves on defence. Faced with an overlap, there is still a rule which holds true more often than not for a winger — stay on the outside and stick with your opposite. To be drawn infield generally provides a free route to the try-line. If you stay out wide, it is fair to assume the cover can always look after the man inside, on the basis that anyone covering has far less distance to travel to the man inside the winger than he does to the man on the outside. However, if it is obvious that there isn't anyone pushing from the inside, a winger has to come in and make a ball-and-all tackle to stop the attacking movement. This requires good timing and judgement.

Coaches have different ideas about the halfback's defensive duties. Some like them in the frontline, mixing it with the forwards and making tackles on them if necessary. Other coaches fancy the halfback patrolling behind the line as a sweeper or second line of defence, ready to cover anyone who breaks through.

Another integral part of the defensive strategy today is using the interchange bench. In certain situations, it makes sense to take a big ball-playing prop off and bring on a work-rate forward if you've been subjected to a few sets of tackles on deep defence.

Effective tackling is needed to make a defence work to its optimum, but much of the work is done if there is first an appropriately thought-out and well-managed defensive pattern.

Following pages: In modern league, there is an acceptance that players ought to be interchangeable and mark off against anyone. But Western Suburbs were defensively at fault when halfback Steve Georgallis was left to handle hard-running Warriors prop Hitro Okesene — that is not a little man's job.

RICSSON

ANSETT
7

ATTACK

If I could get my players to master the simplest of plays —
the fancy stuff was a piece of cake.

Jack Gibson (legendary Australian coach)

Opposite: He became the subject of a protracted contract wrangle after signing with both the Warriors and Canberra, but centre Ruben Wiki boosted the Raiders' already rich reservoir of attacking talent in 1994. To play for Canberra is to know what it means to attack.

Rugby league is like any sport — it lives or dies as a spectacle through its attacking qualities. That is the way supporters judge it, and so do players and coaches. It is true that games can be won solely through defence; a side which mounts a tight defensive pattern built around hard-hitting tackling is able to force opponents into making mistakes. And from those errors alone, sides will continue to win games. But it is not a rewarding way to play rugby league; it goes against the philosophy of the game to play it so defensively. Some coaches want it that way, but it deprives players of a fair degree of personal enjoyment, not to mention the paying public, which is entitled to expect more entertainment than games stifled of action by defensive tactics.

Of course, rugby league can't be played with attack as the only consideration. That is just not realistic. Attack involves an element of risk and risks taken often create errors, so a side with an attack-at-any-cost attitude will be punished. At the same time,

Right: Warriors loose forward Tony Tuimavave has reinforcements on attack against Western Suburbs. While his first interest is to throw the ball to a runner on his right, second rower Stephen Kearney has given him the inside option. Kearney is screaming for ball, ready to provide the alternative route of attack if needed.

all players need to be alert to the chance to launch an attacking raid, even from the deepest defence. If you watch league sides, you will soon detect those that are programmed to play only the percentages and those that aren't.

In many teams, the fullback's job on fielding a kick near his goal-line, or behind it, is simply to run the ball back as far as he can. He'll never look to pass the ball to a supporting player; even when the attacking side has failed to put on a good chase, and a pass to an unmarked winger could gain valuable metres. That is just the way it is for a side run by a 'no-risks' coach.

Some players, like those of the calibre of Phil Blake, consider all the options. They vary their approach; sometimes picking up a supporting winger, other times running the ball back when

The secret on attack is to have the line set deep. That's just what Canterbury-Bankstown have done and, typically in the modern game, the man at first receiver about to catch the ball is the halfback, in this case Craig Polla-Mounter. In just about every top-level side today, it is the halfback who is the pivot of the attack. He controls and dictates play.

there is nothing else on. Phil Blake sometimes uses his exceptional pace to scoot across field in an attempt to outflank the defence. North Sydney's Matt Seers and Canberra's Brett Mullins are much the same with their scorching pace.

With Blake, Seers and Mullins, you have fullbacks with an attacking mentality even on deep defence; players who will take what can usually be regarded as calculated risks and won't play it straight every time. These types of players create uncertainty for any defence trying to contain them or close them down.

There are also plenty of teams which will hardly ever vary the way they play every set of six tackles in possession, especially inside their own half. It might be a case of the fullback or one of the wingers running back a kick on the first, with the dummy

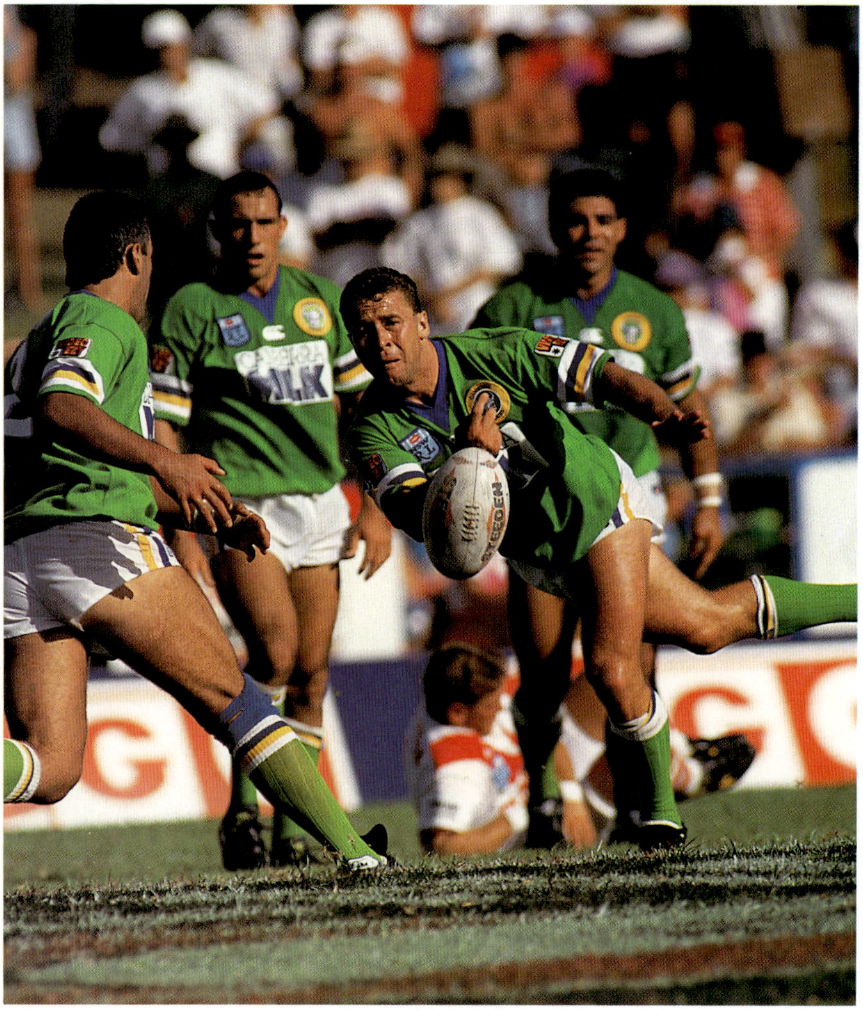

To have a coaching philosophy which encourages attack is not enough on its own, there must be some players of quality in a team to turn a side into a potent attacking force.

Left: In Ricky Stuart Canberra have a halfback who can orchestrate an attack better than any other player in the game at the moment. Stuart's trick is that his passing and kicking game boasts such variety.

Opposite: But Canberra's attacking panache needs more than playmakers like Ricky Stuart and Laurie Daley, it also needs gamebreakers, exceptional talents who can finish off their creations, and even do some creating themselves. In that category file Canberra fullback Brett Mullins as one of the best. He is an exceptionally gifted runner and ball player.

half having a dab on the second. On the third, fourth and fifth tackles there might be another dummy half run with the other two tackles involving nothing more complicated than the forwards hitting the ball up but never passing. Then on the last tackle, it is always the kick option, put on a good chase and try and force the opposition into error.

This is the ultimate in what is called 'one-out football', where the ball is rarely moved more than one off the ruck (that is, the ball is passed only by the dummy half to a player stationed closest to him, otherwise known as the first receiver). The theory is, if the ball is passed as few times as possible it minimises the risks. Even in the attacking half of the field, such teams play it that way and will consider moving the ball along the line only when a try is a near certainty.

Naturally, such an attacking approach is much easier to defend against. The trouble is the game itself does suffer at times because

Above: Great Britain second rower Denis Betts turns the attacking screws on the Kiwis at Wembley in 1993. He's drawing both Tony Kemp (left) and Stephen Kearney in to him, knowing he has support available on his right.

some coaches and teams still have success through such basic and unimaginative tactics; so there will always be coaches who persevere with it. It will win a share of games but fortunately it doesn't often bring home the ultimate prizes.

The success of Canberra and Brisbane in Australia and Wigan in England has merely served to underline the reality that teams with the best attacks — backed by sound defence — take the titles. From 1989–94, the Raiders won the Winfield Cup three times, the Broncos twice with Canberra preventing a clean sweep only when they lost the 1991 grand final to Penrith. In that same period, Wigan won the English first division and the Challenge Cup each year, proving class nearly always prevails in rugby league '90s style.

Assuming you have the necessary ingredients in your playing personnel — namely players with obvious talent and skill as well as pace — all sides need an expansive attacking policy.

Top right: The Warriors mount the perfect attacking raid. Captain Dean Bell has unloaded the ball in the tackle to his stand-off Gene Ngamu, leaving a Western Suburbs defender out of commission on the turf, and Warriors fullback Phil Blake is right there to back up the break.

Bottom right: Again the attacking numbers stack up well for the Warriors. Brisbane prop Glenn Lazarus is well out of the action as Gene Ngamu shifts the ball knowing he has support.

Even the rules now encourage it; the 10-metre rule (the defending team must line up 10 metres back from the play the ball) provides huge scope to organise moves and get the ball wide.

Some attacks come unstuck when teams try to move the ball once too often, perhaps when the pass is not really on, especially early in the tackle count. While it is good to have the confidence to use the football, judgement is vital. If someone makes a 40-metre or 50-metre break running a kick back from defence, the temptation is there to keep the ball moving to the point of throwing a speculative pass; when that happens, it is criminal. If the pass is on and the support is there, fine, go for it. But if there is any doubt, it is always better to take the tackle; after all, you still have the ball for five more tackles and, if you have busted a side open with a 50-metre break, it is fair to assume the defence will be sufficiently disorganised that a try might present itself on the next tackle, or the third or fourth. It is simply a case of respecting possession when you have it.

The same scenario can develop on the third, fourth or fifth tackle. You can string together so many great passes that it becomes almost contagious and, sure enough, one marginal pass is thrown and the chance of a try has gone. There is a fine line between enterprise and carelessness on attack, although the saying about risks shouldn't be forgotten; not taking one is the biggest risk of all.

Crucial to firing any attack is the swiftness and accuracy of your passing game, kicking game and the line of attack, or the way players run with and run onto the ball. (Passing, running and kicking are all covered more specifically in other chapters.)

While attacking play benefits from, and needs, the unexpected provided by players with instinctive flair, it also needs to be structured. Many plays in rugby league don't vary much at all. The success of most moves depends on the fundamentals of having props who hit the ball up strongly on the early tackles, plus a hooker who can scatter the defence with his dummy half running. Momentum must be generated to create the roll-on effect needed on attack.

It is also an absolute necessity to have a proven playmaker at halfback or stand-off in the mould of a Ricky Stuart, Allan Langer, Greg Alexander, Gary Freeman, Cliff Lyons, Jason Taylor, John Simon and Laurie Daley; in England the equivalents are Shaun Edwards, Garry Schofield and Bobby Goulding. They are players who usually control, if not dominate, the attack. It is an even greater advantage to have two quality playmakers in the halves; Canberra have Stuart and Daley, Brisbane look to Langer and Kevin Walters, Manly have Lyons and Geoff Toovey, the Warriors boast Alexander and Gene Ngamu, while in England one of the great combinations used to be that of Edwards and Andy Gregory at Wigan. Players like these are rarely out of the game. There are times when they handle the ball every time in a set of six, generally lining up at first receiver to pick up runners outside or inside them, to take on the defence, to move the ball wide or to kick.

With inside combinations like those at Canberra, Brisbane and elsewhere, teams have all sorts of alternatives on attack and you will find these sides have rather different strategies to many others when in possession. Some teams will use their early tackles to take the point of attack right over to one side of the field. You will notice on tackles one, two and three, they will work only one side of the play the ball or ruck area to bring it close to one touchline. The aim is to drag defenders across to that side of the field and then swing the ball back to the openside

Opposite: Canberra, Brisbane and Wigan stand alone as almost the ultimate sides; they are exceptional on attack and ruthless in defence and they have such depth in star quality. While other sides don't have the same player riches they remain attacking threats because they still have some players with the X Factor.

Top left: So often the kick-start for a sparkling Leeds performance comes from Garry Schofield. Whether he's at halfback or stand-off, Schofield can make the Leeds attack hum, mainly through his vision and ball skills. What you see with him, and all playmakers, is that they run with the ball in two hands.

Top right: Castleford rely on the Kiwi influence, principally from loose forward Tawera Nikau. Again Nikau has immense ball-playing skills, giving Castleford's attack plenty of bite.

Bottom left: While Warrington have Jonathan Davies' wide range of skills, the ball 'whiz' for them has been Kelly Shelford. While not exceptionally quick over a distance, Shelford's fast hands, fast feet and fast mind have had much to do with Warrington's success.

Opposite bottom right: While it is important to have a deep attack, in the sense of having a backline set deep, it is also vital to have depth in attacking numbers. Canberra's Kiwi forward Quentin Pongia has that comfort with Paul Osborne and Steve Walters (right) both backing up his run. Attacking in ones is usually a waste of time.

PUMA

Ellgren

PUMA

CANBERRA
MILK

The playmakers aren't difficult to distinguish in Winfield Cup teams. Not all sides can be as flush with them as Canberra or Brisbane, but there are some outstanding talents.

Left: One of the most obvious is Manly's Cliff Lyons. When he fizzes on attack, Manly are close to unbeatable. Again it's all in the hands; he makes the ball do the work, and just about every time you see him with the ball, he'll have it in both hands.

Right: Greg Alexander used to be the wizard behind Penrith's attack, now he does the same for the Warriors. Running to the defensive line he creates enormous doubt, his kicking game causes constant danger and his passing skills are a joy to behold. If he doesn't make a break or half-break himself, he's sure to back up one made by someone else.

Far right: He doesn't match the formula of the Winfield Cup's typical playmaker. After all, you won't find him popping up at first receiver all the time, orchestrating the attack. But whether he is on the wing or at fullback — and especially at fullback — Kiwi international Jason Williams provides another dimension to the Sydney Bulldogs' attack.

using the whole width of the field on a later tackle.

But sides with two topline playmakers, in the style of Alexander and Ngamu, adopt a different strategy. Early tackles will be used to take the ruck area to around 30 metres infield from either touchline. The aim is to leave two potential channels of attack; one down the so-called short side and the other on the open, with the two playmakers lined up on either side of the ruck. That way you pose a double threat and can have a choice of which way to go.

Ball-playing forwards are also back in vogue now there is so much more latitude offered by the 10-metre rule. If Mark Graham had been a few years younger, he would revel in the room now available because his exceptional running and ball-playing talents would have been given full rein, something which wasn't often possible under the old 5-metre rule. It made an enormous difference to Stephen Kearney at the Warriors. He's the perfect example of the big back row forward you can station two, three or even four men off the ruck where the defence is

not as compressed as it is around the play the ball area. That enables him to use his off-loading skills to put runners into space; good halves will be able to move the ball to him swiftly and, with players backing up inside and outside, he can create mayhem, as can other forwards of his type.

It works the same closer in, too. With the defensive line 10 metres back, props have room to build momentum hitting the ball up, even more so when the defensive line doesn't move up swiftly enough.

But any player in an attacking position needs team-mates to back him up. As communication is a key word on defence, support is a key word in attack. It is very difficult to attack confidently and consistently if players don't back up; support the ball carrier and everything is possible.

The game is full of polished support players — they make a point of being there for the pass. Among those with exceptional reputations for backing up are Terry Lamb, Allan Langer and Gary Freeman. Watch them after they have moved the ball on and they never drift out of the action or lose contact; they are all over the field trying to back up the ball carrier.

In England, Shaun Edwards and Ellery Hanley are the same, although Ellery has slightly different tactics. He doesn't generally pop up on the extremities of the field; his method is to move up the middle, looking to back up a break on the inside. He scores an awful lot of tries that way and was still doing it for Leeds in 1995.

The need for structure on attack has been mentioned, but in some ways the game isn't as structured as it used to be. Wingers, for instance, pop up all over the field now. They have a brief to wander around the field looking for work and attacking chances. Second rowers and props are often stationed wide out on attack. The emphasis is no longer on the old style of props always being lined up in precisely the 'right' spot on every tackle. Positional play is now far more flexible.

As for attacking moves themselves, we could go on forever. There are so many different ones, and too many to run through in this forum. Basic ploys apply in any game, though. The simple run around is one of the most obvious. This is where the receiver takes the ball standing flat and picks up a runner who doubles around him, appearing on the outside to create an overlap.

Decoy runners are very much in force when teams are in possession. They can be used in all sorts of ways, all designed to commit a defender or defenders and create a hole or an overlap as the ball is moved to another player.

Another basic move, used by John Monie, is called 'unders'. When moving the ball along the line, the aim is to pick up a runner who hits the pass running straight or coming back on an angle. It is designed to make the opposition's sliding defence hesitate, or check and change direction, so creating room wider out.

What you need on attack is variety yet simplicity. Complex plays can too often break down, whereas basic moves executed efficiently can cause damage. Variety can come in the form of a healthy collection of moves that the team has practised and is familiar with; maybe there might be one particular move which has several variations on the theme.

Variety can also be more basic. Instead of always putting in a kick on the last tackle, kick on the fourth or fifth tackle, maybe even the second or first if there is a genuine chance of regaining the ball. Look to run the ball on the last tackle sometimes; it is so easy for a defence when a side kicks on the last tackle every time.

Calculated risks are the key to an innovative and successful attack, as are players with talent and a coach who gives them some freedom.

Opposite: Some players have more influence and impact in attack than others, and Brad Fittler is one of them. Whenever Penrith launch an attack, expect him to be one of the key figures.

Following pages: The deep attack again, this time from Illawarra. It's the only way to go for any side with a serious attitude about using the ball on attack.

TER WYNN'S Score
BHP
Steel

AGC

TNT

THE TRY

Teams recover quickly when a flashy individual try is scored against them but they are really flattened when their rivals score after putting together a well-planned move.

Kerry Boustead (Australian International, 1978–84)

The try is the ultimate conquest and statement in rugby league. It is the single reason why the game matters so much to the players; some play to score tries, others are content to make them, still others manage to do both. The quality of touchdowns will vary, at least in the eyes of the purist. There is no great thrill watching a player burrow across the line from dummy half, but there is in seeing a Martin Offiah, Noa Nadruku, Sean Hoppe, Steve Renouf or Brett Mullins scorch 80 metres or more for a try.

There is excitement, too, when a slick move creates a try, and more still when a dazzling sequence of passes and support play climaxes in a try which stuns everyone, the players included. And immediately falling into that category is the incredible try Mark Coyne scored in the 1994 State of Origin series, the one that gave Queensland a 16–12 victory in Sydney after they had trailed 12–4.

Opposite: A four-pointer for Brisbane's Wendell Sailor, but not in the preferred manner. By planting the ball one-handed, Sailor ran the risk of losing control of the ball as he put it down; it could easily have slipped out of his grasp or been knocked loose by a defender.

Right: The sweet feeling of conquest, of out-smarting or over-powering the opposition to put the ball across the try-line. It's the reason footballers play the game. And any try should be savoured, enjoyed and celebrated — the Warriors certainly did when Tony Tatupu (centre) scored against Brisbane. Team-mates Whetu Taewa (left) and Tea Ropati didn't mask their excitement.

Rugby league has produced some astonishing try-scoring machines, and because of the length of the English season and the vast number of matches played, it is there that the most amazing try-scoring records have been achieved.

Left: Former Great Britain captain Ellery Hanley excelled as a player for Wigan, and now Leeds. So much so, that he scored a world record number of tries by a forward in a season, topping the previous mark of 40 in 1994–95. Before becoming a fulltime loose forward, Hanley scored 63 tries for Wigan in the 1986–87 season.

Right: If Hanley has been prolific over a period, then Martin Offiah has had a devastating strike rate since starting in rugby league in 1987. He scored 60 tries in the 1988–89 season and, since shifting from Widnes to Wigan, has maintained an exceptional scoring rate. By the end of the 1993–94 British season, his career showed 325 tries in only 278 matches, most the result of his incredible pace.

Some tries come directly from defensive lapses, such as a bomb spilled near the goal-line or behind it; perhaps a pass dropped near the line; or a loose pass intercepted. That is not counting the missed tackles that lead to tries. Such tries can be easy to score. Sometimes it is a matter of simply falling on a loose ball over the goal-line, or taking a pass right on the line with no defence in sight.

Tries can also be difficult to score — more than difficult. I've seen Ellery Hanley and Martin Offiah create tries you wouldn't have thought possible. That Mark Coyne try last year didn't seem possible for most of its journey. Another I might select in that category would be the one Canberra's replacement forward Steve Jackson scored in extra time in the 1989 Winfield Cup grand final against Balmain. There just didn't seem to be any way he could continue and score that try.

SMITH'S
PUMA

As a player, the quality of tries to the beholder is not an issue, not when the game is being played anyway. If it is a close match and you score four tries to the opposition's three, it doesn't matter at all if yours come from dummy half or taps close to the line. They are all worth four points, and usually six when you've got Frano Botica as your kicker. What must always be encouraged is the scoring of tries. They are the lifeblood of rugby league. That is why they carry a value of four points compared to the two for a penalty or conversion and one for a field goal. The accent must be on putting the ball across the try-line. But while the satisfaction for any team is the fact a try is scored, a genuinely exceptional try will give you that extra lift.

English rugby league boasts prolific try-scorers like Martin Offiah, Ellery Hanley and Shaun Edwards. Down Under the same applies to talents such as Steve Renouf, Brett Mullins and Steve Menzies. But for longevity, no one can quite compete with the mercurial Phil Blake. He started his Winfield Cup career with Manly and graduated through South Sydney, North Sydney, Canberra and St George before joining the Warriors in 1995, making an astounding start by scoring nine tries in the first four matches of the season.

Top left: Phil Blake plants the ball securely over the line, well clear of Brisbane's Kevin Walters.

Bottom left: Against Western Suburbs, Blake had one of the best days of his career. This try, one of his four in the match, coming with a one-handed put-down just before Wests winger Darren Willis arrives.

Opposite: One of Blake's two tries against Illawarra, and no room at all for any doubt about the ball being forced.

Playing for the Warriors in 1995, our very first try in the Winfield Cup was special — it made history. But it was a special try on its own in any case, from the great pass Greg Alexander fed Manoa Thompson, to another good ball Thompson gave Whetu Taewa. Then a great run by Taewa as he beat Willie Carne on the outside, stepped inside Julian O'Neill and gave a superb ball back inside for Phil Blake to score. A magic try; a magic moment.

We managed to put together a lot of fine tries after that first one but I guess the individual effort which astonished everyone was Phil Blake's effort against Western Suburbs. Gene Ngamu and Steve Kearney first provided a couple of good balls, Kearney's pass opening up a huge hole for Blake to dash through. But rather than try to run around the last line of defence, Blake came up with the chip and chase. He won it easily. That, too, was a great try.

Blake did everything right scoring that try. He hit the pass at exceptional pace. His chip kick was perfectly weighted into the in-goal area, and all the more remarkable because he was running in one direction yet was able to chip back the other way. His chase of the kick was perfectly timed and absolutely everything was done at full pace. And, in forcing the ball, he took no risks. He smothered it completely. Faultless.

When scoring tries, some rely on sheer pace; some sheer skill and class; some on strength — then there are players that bring a mixture of all these qualities.

Left: Now-retired Australian and Canberra legend Mal Meninga will live on as one of the most powerful attacking weapons the game has ever seen. Given room to generate momentum, he was an irresistible force near the try-line.

Right: Va'aiga Tuigamala also brought Meninga-like power to rugby league when he quit rugby union to sign with Wigan in 1994. In no time, 'Inga the Winger' had developed into a special rugby league talent — as a centre.

Scoring a try close to the line from dummy half requires a totally different approach. Steve Walters is the champion of dummy half tries. He virtually burrows across like a mole, getting right underneath would-be tacklers.

There are players you sense can score tries just about every time they are given the ball in a position of even slight advantage. Steve Renouf, Brett Mullins, Laurie Daley, Noa Nadruku, Sean Hoppe, Steve Menzies, Martin Offiah and, a few years ago, Ellery Hanley, can do the business from anywhere on the field.

There were a couple of games I played for Wigan I'll never forget. We played Leeds in 1991–92 and beat them 74–6. An amazing score and I was pleased enough to score twice. But Martin Offiah got 10 tries in the same game! Then the next season I had one try as we thrashed Swinton 78–0 — only Shaun Edwards got the perfect 10 that day!

Above right: One of the most thrilling try-scoring machines to emerge in years has been Australian and Canberra fullback Brett Mullins. He's a speed machine in the Martin Offiah mould, only Mullins has more all-round class. He has a lethal swerve and sidestep, unbelievable acceleration and magical ball skills as well. In 1994, he averaged almost a try a game for the Raiders.

For sheer power and presence anywhere from 20 metres to 40 metres out, Mal Meninga was awesome, and quite literally unstoppable at times. The number of tries he scored by battering defenders out of the way was quite amazing. But the man had finesse, too, illustrated in the 1994 Ashes series against Great Britain when he intercepted and ran 60 metres. Then, just as the cover defence moved on him near the line, he instinctively flipped a perfect pass to Andrew Ettingshausen, who had loomed up outside him to score in the corner.

Tries like that, and most tries that are scored, are the culmination of doing so many things right earlier on. They can be the result of a thunderous hit which has jolted the ball loose, instantly turning defence into attack, and a perfectly executed set of six tackles can finish with a try 60 metres or so further down the field. That is when the game is definitely worth it.

Left: Going low. Canberra's Kiwi forward Quentin Pongia burrows across for a rare Winfield Cup try against North Sydney. Close to the line with a wall of defenders in front, the ball carrier's most logical option is generally to drive across low.

Opposite: Few players in the world can quite match the show Martin Offiah puts on after scoring a try. It doesn't matter who it's against, he celebrates. Only this time the celebration was for an even better reason — beating Australia in the first Ashes test in 1994.

Following pages:
When you're built as close to the ground as Allan Langer there is not a long way for the ball to travel in the course of dotting it down for a try.

But finishing the try off is crucial. Some players are still comfortable planting the ball down one-handed, at least when there are no defenders around. It is far better to flop over the line to ground the ball, falling over with it clutched around your chest area. It is also advisable to secure the ball with both arms if you don't need an arm to fend off a defender, or to scramble over the line if you have been knocked off balance just short of it. And it never hurts to look out for the chance to run the ball back around closer to the posts after you have crossed the line, making it easier for the kicker to convert.

As for showmanship after scoring a try, well that is up to the individual. Martin Offiah and Shaun Edwards have their own routines when celebrating a try. You may not be quite that theatrical, but you should enjoy a try when you score it. It is why you play the game, so let it show. Fans love seeing tries scored; players should show they love scoring them.

GREAT BRITAIN
2
17
NIKE

TOOHEYS
TOOHEYS

S LEAS

Above: The spoils of victory. John Monie knows more than most coaches how that feels.

Preceding pages: The reason for playing and the reason he's so good — Sean Hoppe grabs another try.